Don't Steal The Staples

Towards a Better Vision for Faith in the Workplace

Peter Ibison

malcolm down

PUBLISHING

What Others Have Said...

Too often Christianity's teachings are church-centric and rarely equip believers to live out their calling in their day-to-day lives. In this delightful new book, Peter sets out a manifesto for applying one's faith to the workplace, and it has inspired me to better engage with my mission field.
Phillip Dolby, Freelance Journalist and Editor

We spend the majority of our lives in the workplace and our faith in that environment is such an important topic both to us and God. Peter brings challenge and inspirational stories around our identity in Christ. Reading this book has given me a new perspective on my ministry and how God can use me in my workplace.
Lisa Wilson, Teacher

I wish this book had been around 40 years ago when I was starting out as a lawyer – it would have helped me to better understand God's role in my workplace, and may have avoided the burn-out I suffered early on.
David Eastwood, Vicar and Former Lawyer

Great wisdom and insights on who God is, who we are and how that comes together for Christians at work – whatever the context may be. This book is evidently written from a background of years of prayer, reading, learning and actually living out faith through the highs and lows of work.
Sam Evans, Director of Youth and Social Action

As a music teacher in my mid-20s, looking at an imminent career change, I found this book to be full of biblical wisdom and very helpful stories. If you are unsure how God feels about your place of work, or if you are trying to find spiritual meaning for your work, then this book is a must read!
David Butler, Musician and Teacher

Fabulous, easy to read without being superficial, dealing with real issues with a lot of intriguing bite for me. There is some great diving into knotty issues. It should be recommended reading for anyone starting a career who wants to follow the Lord in it!
Mick Rolley, Teacher

It is clear how well thought out and inspired Peter's book is. Not only does it encourage us to think about our daily working lives in a refreshing new way, it reinforces the fact that God is there with us every step of the way, and cares about the work that we do and important life choices that we make. It is challenging to know how to pray and engage with God about our work, but Peter's book reveals the reasons why we should, why it pleases God that we do, and why our daily routine is a vehicle for God's will being done on earth, regardless of our job title. Relevant and sometimes unexpected examples help give a tangible and practical application of how we need not leave God at the door when we leave for work in the morning, but instead engage with him in situations where we might not even think he would have input.
Stephen Coleman, Actuary

Demonstrating a dynamic faith in the workplace can be a huge challenge, but Peter brings together years of experience and deep thought to practically equip us for the adventure. A must read for anyone serious about seeing their faith come alive at work.

Pete Wynter, Leadership Pastor, Holy Trinity Brompton

I used to struggle to see how God could use me in my workplace. Surely God cares more about the work of missionaries or my church leader? Not so! Peter invites us to take on the humbling challenge of adopting a counter-cultural and kingdom-principled mentality – no matter where you work.

Josh Coleman, Lawyer

What a useful book! It contains wonderful insights considering the purpose of God, the presence of God and partnering with God in our secular work. I found it clear, easy to read, encouraging, practical and challenging. I wish I had read it earlier in my career. I especially liked the crafted prayers at the end of each chapter. Thank you, Peter.

Lydia Rolley
Occupational Therapist and Systemic Psychotherapist

Copyright © 2021 Peter Ibison
First published in 2021 by Malcolm Down Publishing Ltd.
www.malcolmdown.co.uk

24 23 22 21   7 6 5 4 3 2 1

British Library Cataloguing in Publication Data
A catalogue record for this book is available from the British Library.

ISBN 978-1-915046-00-0

Cover design by Esther Kotecha
Art direction by Sarah Grace

Printed in the UK

Contents

Introduction

When I started my working life in 1984, I wanted to serve God in my workplace. I had been fortunate enough to receive significant teaching and discipleship in my early years as a Christian but I felt ill-equipped for the rigours of the workplace and my focus therefore tended to be narrow and limited. When I tried to live out my Christian life, my focus was on issues like 'integrity' but this seldom extended beyond the mandate to *'not use workplace resources for personal benefit'* (i.e. *Don't Steal the Staples*). God's purpose and his wisdom for the workplace, which I have been learning since, is so much greater.

I began to write this book in 2018 but I first started asking questions, reading books and attending conferences on the subject twenty years earlier. I've included in a bibliography some of the influences in my thinking over this period but I did not want to summarise the writings of others in the book. I wanted instead to bring fresh insight and to explore areas of faith that I believe have hitherto been little addressed by the Faith at Work Movement.

When I was in hospital for a short period in 2017, I had a profound experience of God in answer to the prayers of friends within my local church. Out of that experience, I started to write this book.

I established three guidelines for myself in writing. I will allow you to judge whether I have been successful, but I want to set out my intentions so they are clear.

❖ I wanted the book to be practical. I did not want to write something that is of theoretical interest alone; I felt it important that those in work would find helpful and practical suggestions as to how to live as a Christian in the workplace.

❖ I wanted the book to be based on unvarnished experience and for the ideas to have been tested in real situations. This was to include 'successes' and 'failures' along the way. I wanted the book to be authentic.

❖ I wanted to listen to what I believe the Holy Spirit is saying to the church today on the subject of faith at work.

The book is written with anyone in mind who works in paid employment or as a volunteer. It is written for professionals and non-professionals; God does not discriminate in these matters. It is written for those at the start of their working life who want input as to what it means to live as a Christian at work. I hope that it will also benefit those at later stages in their working life; confirming experiences or offering an opportunity for meaningful reflection and redirection.

Why is this book important? I believe that in the current literature available there are four gaps.

❖ There are many books written by paid church workers offering helpful insight but few have been written by those working in 'secular' workplaces. I wanted to offer a perspective from someone who works in an environment not always sympathetic to Christian values.

❖ There is little material available that recognises the spiritual battle we face in our places of work; most don't acknowledge it. We know a God whose purposes are good and for our welfare, but there is also an enemy who wants to *steal and kill and destroy* (John 10:10) what God is doing. In each section of the book I have explored this conflict in more detail.

❖ Many books address matters of Christian behaviour (integrity, honesty, justice, etc.) but few also deal with motivation ('*What is God's purpose in work?*') and practice ('*What does this mean for the way in which I do my work?*') I wanted to write in a way that brought these issues together.

❖ Much of the existing material available is written by capable leaders at the *executive level* within their settings. Whilst the stories can be inspiring and lessons worthwhile, I considered that it was important to represent a wider cross-section of settings.

I pray that you find this book useful.

All the stories in this book are about real people (except the fable about stonemasons in Chapter One). In most cases their names and circumstances have been changed to ensure anonymity. In other cases, permission has been granted to share their stories.

Chapter One

Purpose of God in the Workplace

God blessed them and said to them, 'Be fruitful and increase in number; fill the earth and subdue it.'
(Genesis 1:28)

1 Introduction

From the age of twelve, my father instilled within our family the importance of work. Whilst work from such an early age might seem strange to some, and may have even been questionable, I am grateful for that investment. I suspect his desire for us four children stemmed from a range of influences.

He placed a strong value on financial independence and I can recall how, when I eventually left home, he seemed pleased that I had found a job that provided some financial security. A family of four children can do that to you. I suspect that he faced great uncertainty when he was evacuated to the USA in 1943 at the age of twelve. I believe that uncertainty had its impact and affected how he saw his world of work.

For me, throughout my schooling years, a number of part-time jobs followed. I worked at a fish and chip shop skinning fish and removing the inners from chicken in the early hours of each Saturday morning. The work was hard and the environment cold – the main aspect I remember was the abundance of ice about the place, presumably to keep the fish fresh. The job did not last long.

In applying for another job on the Bolton High Street, my father thought it would be a good idea to mention that I had previous experience working at a fish and chip shop. A second job working on the front desk at a second fish and chip shop followed, a job for which I was wholly unsuited.

There were other jobs too: a pet shop, a garage, a bar and then teaching computer skills night classes at a further education college, to name a few jobs before I turned eighteen.

Although I had been brought up in a God-fearing household, it wasn't until I went to university in 1981 that I made a personal profession of faith as a Christian. I graduated in the summer of 1984 from Salford University, proudly holding a degree in Mathematics and Computing primed, to begin work at Ferranti Computer Systems near Manchester, England.

I was excited about work and interested in technology but I had little appreciation of how my newly found faith and my work life might interact. I arrived at work brimming with enthusiasm, sporting a new jacket and driving a rusty second-hand Vauxhall Chevette bought from a friend. My first task was to print listings of computer programs (several hundreds of pages), bind and label them individually. It took six weeks to complete the task. This was a necessary job, but it was boring and uninspiring work – and certainly not what I had in mind when I had finished my university education.

I had no idea then what path my career would follow and what challenges it would present. I have since had the privilege of working in the manufacturing, education, media and telecommunications industries; have worked for over thirty-six years, extended my professional education and have also undergone two redundancies. The desire for faith to impact my work life has remained unaltered throughout, whether the tasks that God has given have been challenging, exciting or even mundane.

And so, having painted a picture of the start of my career, I would like to extend to you an invitation. Imagine for a moment your working life with God at the centre. You are convinced that God has called you to your role and that you have worthwhile work to do. You are assured that God is with you in your daily tasks and in your interactions with others. You have an acute sense of partnering with God as you go about your daily work. That is what I believe God wants for all of us.

Let us start our journey by asking, *'Is God really interested in our places of work?'* The answer to this is important and will influence how we see our work and its impact in our Christian lives.

Few would doubt that God has a plan by the Holy Spirit, to develop our character to become more Christ-like. After all:

The fruit of the Spirit is love, joy, peace, forbearance, kindness, goodness, faithfulness, gentleness and self-control. Against such things there is no law. (Galatians 5:22-23)

The fruit of the Spirit is needed in our workplaces as much as our neighbourhoods, communities and churches. But there is something to be explored prior to that of character, and that is the matter of God's *purpose* for our work. Typically, over a lifetime a person might spend 90,000 hours engaged with work. It would seem strange, therefore, if God's word does not have something to say about his purpose for what is such a large proportion of our waking lives. In this first chapter, I want us to explore in further depth *God's purpose* in our place of work.

2 God's purpose

If we look at God's instruction to Adam in the Garden of Eden we will see that there is both an explicit command to Adam (to fill the earth) but also an unwritten purpose; that of being an image bearer.

2.1 God's purpose is that we be image bearers

God said to Adam:

Be fruitful and increase in number; fill the earth and subdue it. Rule over the fish in the sea and the birds in the sky and over every living creature that moves on the ground. (Genesis 1:28)

Humankind was to procreate and spread far and wide; a command given first to Adam and Eve and later to Noah and his sons; prior to the covenantal relationship with Abram being in place. There has in recent times been much debate about what it means to 'subdue' the earth, especially given contemporary ecological concerns, but we will not look into that here.

God's purpose was that humankind, both male and female, might be *'image bearers'* throughout the earth, ruling over Creation, enjoying God's provision (of fruit and seed) and going about their daily work. Male and female were created in God's image and when they went about their work, that work was designed to bear his hallmark.

We bear the image of God and demonstrate this in the world whenever we show divine characteristics; including creativity, compassion, love, a desire for justice and peace. When we exemplify these in our places of work, our working lives become more fruitful. But this process must start by pursuing godly character.

For example, imagine you work in an organisation where there is one employee who is aloof and generally not well-liked by others in the team. You have observed that many team members steer clear of this individual, finding them difficult, unsociable and abrasive. How do you respond as a Christian? Or put another way, what is the heart of God in this situation? We need to ask ourselves, how can God's character be reflected in our situation?

We need to ask ourselves, how can God's character be reflected in our situation?

Or consider a situation where you have been assigned the workplace task of making a team of employees redundant. The task is painful and you are dreading the conversations, the anger, tears and various reactions that could follow. You are aware of the human resource policies as to how this process needs to be conducted. You are also aware of the legal responsibilities you have. But let us ask another question. What is the heart of God in this situation and how can his character be reflected through this experience which we know will be traumatic? How can we demonstrate God's care of the individual?

Most of us will face a redundancy situation at some point in our career – either making others redundant or being made redundant ourselves

We are each image bearers and as we grow in reflecting the character of God, the *way* we go about our work will change.

2.2 What happens when we ignore God's purpose

Now, with the command to rule over Creation and subdue the earth in mind, let us skip forward a few generations and observe the people of Shinar (a place in the region of Babylonia, in modern-day Iraq) who had discovered a new technology: using brick and tar to make stronger buildings. The Lord was interested in that technology and the use to which it was put.

The Lord was interested in their technologies and the usages to which they were put

We might find in our own age that the technology itself is often neutral, but the usage is not. The Internet, for example, has potential for great good, keeping people connected across the globe. But it is also used to inflict great evil: trafficking, trolling and terrorism. We need to observe and shape the uses to which our innovations are put.

So the Lord came down to see what the people were doing; he came to 'check out' their new technology. We can observe how humankind tried to build upward but despite all their efforts to reach the heavens, the Lord still has to 'come down' to meet them!

In this passage we see God's interest in the work we do. Our role may be as a marketer, teacher, tradesman, public servant, business person or artisan – the Lord is interested in our work, both the technologies we use and the uses to which they are put.

The people of Shinar had put together a plan:

They said to each other, 'Come, let's make bricks and bake them thoroughly.' They used brick instead of stone, and bitumen for mortar. Then they said, 'Come, let us build ourselves a city, with a tower that reaches to the heavens, so that we may make a name for ourselves; otherwise we will be scattered over the face of the whole earth.' (Genesis 11:3-4)

Here we see an alternative purpose that differs from that given to Adam; that they might make a name for themselves and not be scattered. It is, of course, not possible to fill the earth and not be scattered at the same time.[1]

> Whenever we strive to fulfil our own purpose rather than God's, we will find our path blocked with thorns and briers. The desire to make a name for ourselves, to find our eternal significance through work is common to many of us, but it is not God's design for our work.

For the people of Shinar, the Lord confused their language so that they were not able to communicate effectively. Their projects broke down, their plans were frustrated, the work was not completed and the people were scattered over the face of the earth. God desires that people live in unity but that unity must have the right end. The people of Shinar were united in their desire to build a tower as an assault on

---

1. We will look at the subject of the role of personal ambition later in this book.

heaven and they wanted to approach God on their own terms. This was not something that the God of heaven could bless.

The temptation for each of us to seek our eternal significance in our work goes deeper than we might be prepared to admit. I've been praying for over thirty years for my workplace and work colleagues and yet still I find myself drawn to seeking my significance through work. This manifests itself by a striving to complete my work and 'feel satisfied', no matter what. At these times, my endeavours are ultimately about serving my own needs to feel significant and worthwhile; they are not about the God whom I worship or the company I serve. In these or similar circumstances the story of Babel serves to remind us that life goes better when we align our purpose to God's.

Where we find our purpose misaligned with God's, this does not mean that God cannot and will not use our endeavours. The people of Shinar now spoke multiple languages which would eventually lead to their dispersion and their 'filling the earth', as God had intended. God's purpose was fulfilled despite their personal ambitions to 'make a name for themselves'.

We may know in our places of work those who strive out of a deep desire to establish their identity. This striving may manifest itself in 'workaholism', for example. In the process, societal needs are met and the workaholic may excel at their job, but often at the cost of both family relationships and their personal soul-development. The point is this: unless our purpose is aligned with God's, we will have little or no sense of partnership with God and the potential for the greater good will be limited.

For many of us, we may be tempted to establish our identity through our work. Workaholism can be the result

2.3 In work, we are called to work from our identity, not towards it

Our workplace may be an arena where we can model godly character, share our faith with others, administer justice and do good to others. These and other purposes are each covered in Mark Greene's *Fruitfulness on the Frontline*.[2] The more we connect with and align our own thinking with God's purpose in our work, the more effective we will be in our jobs.

Consider the story of the three stonemasons who were asked by a passer-by, what work they were doing.

---

2. Greene, Mark, *Fruitfulness on the Frontline: Making a Difference Where You Are* (IVP, 2014).

We will be more effective when we understand how our work aligns with God's purpose

The first answered that they were building a wall. The second said they were working to pay for their mortgage and put food on the table (a noble cause, but not the primary purpose). The third had a broader vision – that of building a cathedral to reflect the glory of God and inspire others in worship.

We will be more effective as workers when we understand our work's purpose and understand how it fits with God's purpose for humankind. The third stonemason maintained the broader vision of their work and this was a conscious choice.

What, might we ask, does God's purpose look like if we are not building a cathedral and our work is as a decorator, accountant, teacher, job recruitment agent or operations manager?

The answer to that question comes from the realisation that we do not work to establish our sense of worth (a very tempting but ultimately counterfeit purpose). We work *from* our sense of worth, bearing the image of God in all we do – and *bringing the presence of God into our work*. The presence of God and the purpose of God are inextricably linked. The greater our appreciation of the former, the more we will understand the latter. God's purpose in our work is that we are *aware of his presence in our work, that we exercise godly character in our places of work* and that we *partner with him in our work*; ultimately that we work for his glory and pleasure.

We can choose to make a name for ourselves in our work but any such gains will be short-lived and hollow. Real joy can be found only where we work *from our identity*. This is harder than we imagine because in order to work from our identity, we need to look inward and ask ourselves who we really are.

So, what are some characteristics of a person who works in order to establish their identity? My thoughts are given in the table opposite. You can, of course, agree, disagree or add your own.

Working from our identity	Working towards our identity
• **Criticism:** We receive criticism from others, weigh it carefully and are able to take the benefit without feeling undermined.	• **Criticism:** We receive criticism from others and it wounds us deeply, yielding little benefit or learning.
• **Reward:** We appreciate reward and recognition but it does not change how we value ourselves. We are confident in how God sees us.	• **Reward:** We feel unvalued and feel annoyed if our work is not well rewarded and recognised.
• **Failure:** We use failure to learn lessons for the future to improve our performance. We can and do talk to God about it.	• **Failure:** We feel angered by failure and often look to apportion blame to causes outside ourselves.
• **Acknowledgement:** We rest in the knowledge that our value and honour come from God and we do not devote time or effort to bolster others' opinion of us.	• **Acknowledgement:** We spend a lot of time positioning our work so that it is acknowledged by others. We get annoyed when others receive plaudits for their work.

I am past the mid-point of my career as I write this. I find that now I am more confident in who I am, the authority I have, and the contribution I bring to my place of work. Some of this has come from experience of over thirty-five years of working life; I know what I can do well and I know many of my weaknesses and how best to address them – I have more self-knowledge than I did at the start of my career. Some of the confidence I have now comes from the suitability of my current role. But mostly, I believe it comes from the work God has done within me in showing me who I am in Christ.

Let us recognise, then, that when it comes to a reliable foundation for our identity, we are called not to look at our gifts and calling but to look heavenwards. The question then becomes not '*What are my strengths?*' or '*What is my role and contribution?*' but '*Who am I in Christ?*', '*How does God view me?*' and '*What is my value to him?*'

If our work flows from our secure position in relation to God, it will have a different quality. Much more of our security therefore needs to be vested in our identity as a beloved son or daughter of God.

This, you might say, sounds too abstract. Let me assure you it is very practical. I've been made redundant twice in my career. On the first occasion, my confidence hit rock bottom and I felt devasted. The exit was abrupt and felt brutal. Overnight I appeared to lose many of my friends and work colleagues. Additionally, I began to question my competence in almost every area of work. I felt deep stress, anxiety and despair coupled with financial worries that affected my family and our future. It was there that I learned something more of the Lord as my '*refuge and strength, an ever-present help in trouble*' (Psalm 46:1).

> **Ultimately there is only one secure foundation and this is in Christ himself. It might take life's setbacks to recognise this truth, or the Lord may teach us through other means. Either way, as we begin to learn our true identity, then our work will flow from that identity and it will have a better quality.**

When our work flows from our identity, this frees us to focus on other aspects of our faith.

There is one final question concerning our identity that I would like to address. God gave personkind a mandate to fill the earth and to rule.[3] Does exercising this mandate contribute *in any way* towards our identity? Or expressed another way, does the work we do make us fuller, more complete and whole individuals? I believe the answer has to be a resounding 'no'. Exercising God's mandate can help to make our lives more productive, fruitful, joyful and fulfilling but it does *not* change our God-given identity. Such an identity is fixed and unchanging. From day to day, our realisation of who we are may ebb and flow, but the reality is unchanging. We are created in the image of God and, as Christians, redeemed by the love and sacrifice of Christ for a new life with God. That is who we are.

2.4 Work as a means of transformation

What we believe about the created universe (and our world) will affect our behaviour. If we believe that the world will ultimately be destroyed at Christ's return to earth, then this will inevitably lead us towards an approach where we use and exploit the world for our own purpose with little regard to sustainability. If we believe that the world will continue but in renewed form, then we are more likely to see our role as stewards.

In other words, what we believe about the end times, will affect our attitude and action towards Creation. The same is true of the workplace, although we might not have consciously thought about it. Some may see our work efforts in this life as only being relevant in shaping the outcomes in the next life. In other words, work is seen

---

3. See Genesis 1:28.

mainly as a vehicle as a context for evangelism. Others will see our work efforts in this life as being transformative in ushering in God's kingdom *in this life*.

Space does not permit a deep analysis of the doctrinal issues around the end times. However, it is worth making the observation that if we work for the transformation of society, then this not only blesses Creation but it creates a climate where kingdom values of truth, integrity, kindness and love are seen and realised. In this sense, we are partners with God is seeing his kingdom rule ushered in.

Let us make this practical. Ask yourself, what is God's vision for your work? Lucy teaches mathematics at a nearby secondary school. The difference she can make in students' lives is incalculable. She helps them realise their dreams, she equips them with skills suitable for their future careers, and she communicates respect, valuing them individually as well as showing patience and good humour.

Sometimes we can make a difference in the lives of others without realising how it positively impacts God's purpose

The point being that her role is transformative for the betterment of others' lives – and in this God takes delight and pleasure. The same is true of each of us. Our impact in the workplace is designed to be transformative.

Veith notes:

> *God calls people to different kinds of labor as part of His governance of the world. God himself is operative in human labor, through His providential power. Though human beings tend to be oblivious to the spiritual significance of the ordinary*

things they do . . . the Christian, walking by faith and resting in
Christ, can live and work as a channel for the gifts of God.[4]

Let's take a commercial role. Alan is a businessman who employs several hundred accountancy staff across South East Asia. His accountancy organisation helps ensure other businesses operate ethically and professionally. He works closely with the national governments in the region to establish standards so that businesses can operate with confidence in their trading relationships. Without his contribution, some local businesses would operate illegally and, ultimately, individuals would be cheated out of their earnings and savings. With his contribution, truthfulness and integrity are much more commonplace.

In both roles, God's purpose is furthered and this does not depend on his using Christian channels to do so.

> God delights in all efforts that maintain kingdom values; even if his sovereignty is not acknowledged by those who work on his behalf.

2.5 The Ten Commandments inform our thinking as to how to fulfil God's purpose of transformation

In addition to us bearing God's image and transforming society, God often uses the work environment to fashion within us

---

4. Taken from *God at Work* by Gene Edward Veith Jr. Copyright © 2021, p. 65. Used by permission of Crossway, a publishing ministry of Good News Publishers, Wheaton, IL 60187, www.crossway.org.

increased Christlikeness. Work is the anvil on which our character is shaped. Certainly this process involves issues of integrity, morality, trustworthiness and much more besides.

The Ten Commandments have a role in shaping our character and how we think about our places of work. Broadly, we could consider four alternative perspectives with regards to the Ten Commandments and their role in the lives of 21st-century Christians. I invite you to consider which most aligns with your own perspective.

i.   **Universally applicable**: The Ten Commandments are seen as applicable for all people; both those inside and outside the church. They are the Maker's instructions and the blueprint designed to bless and govern our lives. We are therefore all required to obey them and blessings flow from our obedience. Grace, of course, is given to Christians when we confess our failures.

ii. **Applicable only when reinforced in the New Testament**: The Ten Commandments are part of an Old Testament covenant relationship with the Jewish people so that the world might see how best to live. Christians are required to live by them only where the Commandments are explicitly reinforced or restated in the New Testament. Outside of these reinforced statements in the New Testament, Christians live in freedom.

iii. **No longer applicable for Christians**: The Ten Commandments are seen as not applicable at all. They are part of the Old Covenant which has since been replaced or superseded by the law of love. Christians therefore are at liberty to be governed solely by this law of love; to love God with all our hearts, minds, soul and strength and to love our neighbours as our self.

iv. **Serve to show us how to love**: The Ten Commandments not only show the best way to live, but they *reflect the heart of God*. They show us *how* to love our neighbour; they show us what love looks like. The New Testament commands to love God and our neighbour can therefore be better understood by reflecting on the Ten Commandments and applying them to our circumstances. This applies as much to Christians as it did to the Jewish race.

So how does this relate to our places of work? An early question I had to ask in my managerial career was what to do when another colleague complained about the performance of a member of my team. What do I do with this information and how do I deal with it in a clear, fair and loving way to a member of my team, whilst at the same time making sure the team member felt supported?

We all will inevitably face difficult conversations at work

Many management books and learning through an MBA have given me input which has helped in part to tease out the principles at stake. But what has made the most impression in shaping my convictions has been my own experience, the love I received from the Lord – and also how my own bosses have treated me. Whilst I've had some really good experiences and some poor ones, I have found both experiences to be valuable with regards to my learning.

The core question at the heart of the issue is "How do I love my work colleague as myself?" and "How do I exercise the God-given mandate to care and rule?"

There are, of course, no easy answers but the point I want to make is that Scripture plays a crucial part in shaping our convictions and, if we are open to him, the Holy Spirit helps in showing us the application of those scriptural principles. Scripture needs to be understood and applied in the workplace. This takes time and diligent effort. It requires a continual measuring of one's own actions and beliefs against those laid out for us in the Bible, including the Ten Commandments.

I believe there is a danger of Christians exercising a superficial application of Scripture in the place of work. I've seen godly Christians who in the church setting are kind, considerate, patient and wise but operate a managerial ruthlessness when in the work context. At this point, some may object and refer to the fact that in the workplace we operate in a different culture and therefore different circumstances apply. Whilst this is true, we need to allow Scripture to shape our convictions and workplace practices. We are each called to be counter-cultural and to apply the principles of Scripture *wherever we are* and whatever the cost. This indeed calls for wisdom as we consider how those principles apply in our places of work.

> God's purpose is at least twofold. He desires that our *character* be transformed in our workplaces as we apply the principles of Scripture, including the Ten Commandments, to our lives. God also seeks the transformation of our *workplaces themselves* into environments where kingdom values are respected and where kingdom blessings follow.

Finally, let us remember that Scripture has much to say about fruitfulness. For instance:

This is to my Father's glory, that you bear much fruit, showing yourselves to be my disciples. (John 15:8)

In evangelical circles, a common understanding is to see fruitfulness in terms of 'people becoming Christians'. And so we understand the verse to mean that God's primary design is that our lives bear fruit in terms of seeing others come to a saving faith in Jesus Christ (i.e. conversions).

Whilst conversion is certainly one aspect of fruitfulness, I do not believe it ends there; fruitfulness is much more besides and involves us also becoming more like Christ in character, exhibiting the fruit of the Spirit in our lives and having a kingdom impact on our workplace environment.

When Jesus spoke to the disciples about fruitfulness, he used the metaphor of the sower. The seed of God's word, when sown in receptive and obedient hearts, produces a crop that is thirty, sixty and a hundred-fold (Matthew 13:23). This multiplication effect will be evident when we live out the principles of God's word in our places of work. Great fruit will follow to the extent we are willing and obedient to live according to God's word.

2.6 God's vision for our workplace

So, before we move on to look at humankind's purpose in the workplace, let us summarise what we have covered with regards to God's purpose. Or put another way, what do we believe is God's vision for our places of work? Much of this is addressed by Mark Greene in *Fruitfulness on the Frontline*[5] but the key elements are as follows.

- **Worship**: God's vision for our workplace is foremost that we glorify him by the way we do our work; that we offer it to him as an act of worship. Our work activities might not change but what will be different is the way we do our work and for whom we work.

  Whatever you do, work at it with all your heart, as working for the Lord, not for human masters. (Colossians 3:23)

- **Transformation**: God's vision is that we experience character transformation in our places of work, as the Holy Spirit continues his work of sanctification in our lives.

  Continue to work out your salvation with fear and trembling, for it is God who works in you to will and act according to his good purpose. (Philippians 2:12-13)

- **Kingdom impact**: God's vision is that we make an impact for God's kingdom. God's kingdom is extended where there is an extension of his rule on earth. This extension can take the form of people

---

5. Greene, Mark, *Fruitfulness on the Frontline: Making a Difference Where You Are* (IVP, 2014).

becoming Christians through the process of evangelism. It can also take the form of kingdom *values* being lived out in our workplaces. God takes delight *wherever* this happens. These values encompass matters like pay, recognition, attitudes of service towards customers, respect for colleagues, matters of integrity and so on.

Mary Gentile explores in her book *Giving Voice to Values* the opportunity we each have to speak up when our personal values and those of our workplace are in conflict. We may choose to be selective as to when we do this but in my own experience, our speaking up is more effective wherever an organisation fails to be consistent with its *own* espoused set of values.

Kingdom impact is not restricted to words. We can have kingdom impact whenever we choose to live in counter-cultural ways. I have found that the Lord has often challenged my own values first as part of this process – how I treat my work colleagues, how I relate to those in authority and the respect I afford others in my workplace.

Finally, you might ask the question, *'Where are my own Christian values and those of my organisation in conflict?'* This may not be immediately apparent to us. I have found a better question to ask is, *'What in my organisation do I really care about?'* This often uncovers a core value or deeply held belief – and is a good starting point for identifying where the Lord invites us to have kingdom impact.

2.7 God's purpose includes all our work, not just part of it

I believe that God has a purpose for all our working lives, not just parts of it. Reflect for a moment on the earlier question: is God really interested in all our working lives? I suggest there are only three broad possible answers.

i. **God is not interested in our work and the real 'battle ground' for our lives lies elsewhere.** Work is purely a means to an end – providing both sustenance and resources to enable the 'real work of God through the church' to continue. This position has little biblical support, yet many of us behave as if we believe it to be true!

ii. **God is interested in our work solely as a means of Christian witness.** Work has no inherent value in itself. The workplace is purely an arena where Christians can be *'salt and light'* (Matthew 5:13-14) in the hope that others might be drawn into the kingdom as they follow Jesus Christ. This position is only partly true. The workplace does provide an arena for Christian witness, but that is not its only purpose.

iii. **God is interested in all aspects of our working lives.** Work has intrinsic value in itself. It is designed, as we work in *partnership with God,* to contribute towards the betterment of society and is God's means of providing for humankind. The farmer plants seeds and cultivates the ground; God provides the rain and crop growth. This *partnership* may not always be acknowledged, but it is always in evidence.

I hope at this point you are persuaded that God's purpose includes *all our work* and not just part of it.

2.8 God's redemptive work

Finally, I want to explore an approach concerning 'redemption'. When Scripture uses the word 'redemption' it is written to describe the fact that God will at the end times transform our bodies to be conformed to that of his Son, Jesus.

We ourselves, who have the firstfruits of the Spirit, groan inwardly as we wait eagerly for our adoption to sonship, the redemption of our bodies. (Romans 8:23)

But what if the process of redemption is also on-going? I have begun to consider in recent years that God wants to transform, or reclaim, *all strata of society*. The aim is to revisit on us a world of kingdom values, where every aspect of our world enjoys the blessing of God's original design.

For example, Stephanie works as a nutritionist with over twenty years' experience in her field. Her work blesses people by offering the best scientific advice and consultations on what to eat.

Our work can have a redemptive quality as it impacts others' lives

Taking this a step further, what if, when people heed that advice, they take a step closer to God's original design for how the body was meant to function? It may be a single step, but if the advice is sound, the effects will be noticed as the person begins to function as God first intended (i.e. they approach closer their Eden origin). When they heed the advice, there will be a 'ring of truth' about it; an echo of Eden. In this sense, her work is *redemptive* since in part, it helps restore the harmony that had previously been lost.

I invite you to measure this theory against Scripture and I believe it can offer fresh perspectives on the value of our work to God's purpose.

2.9 Summary

So let us summarise the key points so far:

❖ God has made us in his image and we are called to bear that image wherever we are, including in the workplace.

❖ God has a purpose and vision for our work and the more we align with his purpose, the more guaranteed will be the resulting fruit. God's purpose is generic in that it applies equally to all of us. God's vision for our places of work will be specific; however, it is personal to us and our specific workplace setting.

❖ Many of us seek to find purpose, significance and identity in our work but this is not God's design. His purpose is that we work *from* a place of significance, not towards it. In fact, we bring significance to our work rather than work giving us significance.

❖ Work presents an opportunity for transformation of God's world too; as we serve, we act as instruments of God's grace in the lives of others.

❖ God is transforming our character in the workplace so that we become more like Jesus. The Ten Commandments inform our thinking so that we better understand the heart of God; his blueprint for how best to live.

3 Humankind's purpose

We have looked at God's purpose in our places of work. Let us now turn to humankind's purpose. We might ask, '*What is the value of such an exercise?*' Surely we need only to understand God's purpose and follow that. However, I would maintain that there is value in looking at our own strivings for purpose in work because it is common to all humankind. As we understand more of this dynamic, we not only understand where we are on our own journey but we will be better placed to empathise with others.

3.1 Humankind searches for purpose, but this is often elusive

We each might strive to find purpose in what we do, quite apart from God. If we seek purpose in our work without a relationship with God at its centre, we will find this purpose elusive. God designed it that way. It is not that God created the frustration or that he is a kill-joy. Rather, the frustration we experience stems from the fact that when we look for purpose, we look in all the wrong places. Ultimately, our souls will only find rest in relationship with the eternal God. Work on its own is a poor substitute.

Solomon wrestled with the question of purpose in the book of Ecclesiastes when he declared that satisfaction in our work is a gift from God, but elusive to him personally. In the passage that follows, observe the job roles that are covered (with a little poetic licence). . .

I wanted to see what was good for people to do under the heavens during the few days of their lives. I undertook great projects [project

management]: I built houses for myself [property development]
and planted vineyards [landscape cultivation]. I made gardens
and parks and planted all kinds of fruit trees in them [landscape
gardening]. I made reservoirs to water groves of flourishing trees
[water engineering] . . . I also owned more herds and flocks
than anyone in Jerusalem before me [farming]. I amassed silver
and gold for myself [stocks and shares management], and the
treasure of kings and provinces . . . I became greater by far than
anyone in Jerusalem before me. In all this my wisdom stayed
with me. I denied myself nothing my eyes desired; I refused my
heart no pleasure. My heart took delight in all my labour, and
this was the reward for all my toil. Yet when I surveyed all that
my hands had done and what I had toiled to achieve, everything
was meaningless, a chasing after the wind; nothing was gained
under the sun. (Ecclesiastes 2:3-11)

Just like Solomon centuries before us, when we look for purpose in
our work apart from God, we will find it to be elusive.

3.2 Elusiveness can be a benefit, but only if we reflect on it

Let us venture a little further. A desire for purpose in your work may
not be a bad place to be, however. We have already seen that God has
placed 'eternity in our hearts'.

He has made everything beautiful in its time. He has also set
eternity in the human heart; yet no one can fathom what God
has done from beginning to end. (Ecclesiastes 3:11)

We long for purpose and that desire can lead us on a journey to
seek his *presence*. If that desire for purpose is foremost in our minds,
then let us journey with the Spirit of God. Wrestle with the desire

Unless we pause to reflect, we may find ourselves climbing a ladder to nowhere

As Christians, the Scriptures show us the wisdom of pausing to reflect. Solomon did such a thing.

> *There was a man all alone; he had neither son nor brother. There was no end to his toil, yet his eyes were not content with his wealth. 'For whom am I toiling,' he asked, 'and why am I depriving myself of enjoyment? This too is meaningless – a miserable business!'* (Ecclesiastes 4:8)

Solomon had personally experienced the frustration of working without finding purpose. He then observed that same predicament in others. He observed a friendless man who had nothing to show for his endeavours. The question *'For whom am I toiling?'* is not so much *'Why are others getting the benefits of my labour?'* but *'Why aren't I realising those benefits myself?'* Or in other words, he was mourning the lack of purpose in his work.

So there is merit in such a reflection, not only observing our own experience of working life but also noting the experience of others we see around us.

My wife once commented to me about her time in her first job outside Oxford. She described her own observations of work colleagues as follows:

There were some work colleagues who clearly worked hard and I'm sure had the expectation of great things through their work. In the end I could see a few despairing men who had worked slavishly but then come to the realisation that much of their efforts had not yielded the expected return. They were disillusioned. Then I also met some Christians and the difference I saw was palpable. These men and women lived for 'now'. They had a future and a hope that was sealed. Their work mattered to them and they enjoyed it, but it didn't define who they were.

The benefit of such reflection is that it orientates us in our thinking towards a more guaranteed hope and purpose.

3.3 Humankind looks for purpose in work

The fact that Solomon, in all his wisdom, was unable to find purpose in his work does not mean that it cannot be found in part. If we look around and see our work colleagues, some would say that they find their work fulfilling. I will, however, suggest an alternative approach to looking for purpose from our work.

There may be occasions where we find meaning and fulfilment in our work – and there may be some types of work that are inherently more satisfying than others. But what if we look at it another way? Work is not really designed to bring meaning to an 'otherwise meaningless existence'. That is not work's purpose. We are, instead, designed to *bring meaning to our work* by virtue of God's image within us and by our working in partnership with him. We bear God's image and his Spirit lives within us. We are designed to bring meaning to our work rather than the other way round.

This can be illustrated as follows:

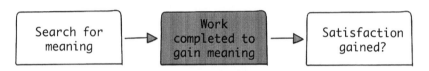

A typical approach to searching for purpose

Typically, humankind searches for meaning and uses work as a vehicle to find meaning. Satisfaction can result but it is not guaranteed; it is elusive.

Alternatively, as Christians we may choose to reflect the image of God in and through our work. As we offer our work as an act of worship, God is glorified and our relationship with God grows stronger and deeper. Satisfaction and fulfilment are often the result. God's favour is guaranteed.

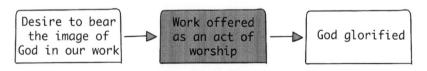

A more biblical approach

After an extensive search for meaning, Solomon concluded his personal journey with this statement:

Now all has been heard; here is the conclusion of the matter: fear God and keep his commandments, for this is the duty of all mankind. (Ecclesiastes 12:13)

Solomon had established that the longings within the human heart were placed there by God, that purpose in our work is a gift from God and that human strivings to find purpose in our work apart from God will prove fruitless. He then concludes in his final chapter that our sole responsibility is to *'fear God and keep his commandments'* (Ecclesiastes 12:13). Solomon was saying that the search for purpose in our work, without God, is a dead end; a cul-de-sac.

> **We have an alternative open to us as Christians where we bear the image of God, offer our work as an act of worship and seek to glorify God in our work. If we do this then we will find that purpose is a by-product along the journey.**

Let us conclude this section with a word of encouragement for those who have offered their work as an act of worship to God and yet still feel a sense of despair in their work. The final step in the process (God glorified) may not be immediate and suffering may be a part of our experience. Scripture offers encouragements: our labour is not in vain and our suffering will pass. Paul said to the Corinthian church:

Therefore, my dear brothers and sisters, stand firm. Let nothing move you. Always give yourselves fully to the work of the Lord, because you know that your labour in the Lord is not in vain. (1 Corinthians 15:58)

And the apostle Peter reminds us:

And the God of all grace, who called you to his eternal glory in Christ, after you have suffered a little while, will himself restore you and make you strong, firm and steadfast. (1 Peter 5:10)

3.4 Humankind looks for work to endure

For many of us, we search for meaning by investing in work that has longevity – the longer our work endures, we conclude, the greater will be our satisfaction in our work. How many monuments are erected in our towns and cities with this same purpose?

Much of our work will, however, last only for a short season. An accountant might prepare end-of-year accounts that after six years are shredded.

Some of our work may only last a short period here on earth

A teacher's work will last a little longer, affecting a child's life and prospects. A tradesman might fix a plastering problem and the newly installed plasterwork could endure for say fifty years or more. The seasons may vary in length but in our souls we may still find there is restlessness. We were designed for eternity not for twenty years or more; eternity is our home and our heritage. Anything that is temporary in effect will feel insubstantial in comparison.

Whilst the work we do is temporal – we can find that its effects have eternal impact

Cosden explores the idea that our earthly work will endure in heaven and on the new earth.[6] Much of his analysis is based on the example of Jesus. His earthly work involved suffering and dying on the cross before being raised from the dead. Cosden notes that the nail-pierced hands are still in evidence in his resurrected body. In other words, there were elements of Jesus's finished work on earth that were carried over into his resurrection state. He then suggests that what is true of Jesus may also be true of our work. It is an attractive theory that would go some way to giving eternal relevance to our earthly work activities. But is it biblical?

Scripture is clear that our work will be rewarded and will in some sense 'survive'. Paul wrote, for example, to the Corinthian church to explain that elements of his work would be rewarded, depending on the quality of that work:

---

6. Cosden, Darrell, *The Heavenly Good of Earthly Work* (Paternoster Press, 2006).

For we are fellow workers in God's service; you are God's field, God's building. By the grace God has given me, I laid a foundation as a wise builder, and someone else is building on it. But each one should build with care. For no one can lay any foundation other than the one already laid, which is Jesus Christ. If anyone builds on this foundation using gold, silver, costly stones, wood, hay or straw, their work will be shown for what it is, because the Day will bring it to light. It will be revealed with fire, and the fire will test the quality of each person's work. If what has been built survives, the builder will receive a reward. (1 Corinthians 3:9-14)

Paul co-laboured with God in building into people's lives. If this work was pursued for selfish aims (self-aggrandisement for example) then it would not have endured nor have been rewarded. However, Paul's words inform us that work done for God's glory will endure. This is certainly true of the missional work in which Paul was engaged. People became Christians and this work ensured that Paul would be able to greet those same converts in heaven. In other words, Paul would see the fruit of his labours in eternity.

But it does not end there. Other work will be included in God's ultimate purpose. If God's purpose is a rich tapestry being worked out over history, we each have a role to play. Those individual efforts, those threads – which include our work endeavours given to our Lord – can be used for his purpose. We may not see the tapestry in this life but we can choose to trust God that our work *in the Lord* is not in vain.

Ultimately, our work, offered as an act of worship to God, will bring reward in the life beyond this one. The work itself may have lasting properties into the next life and our eternal reward is a certainty.

3.5 Humankind looks for identity in work but this is a frail foundation

The book of Genesis tells the story of Joseph, a young man of seventeen years. He was his father's favourite and, because he was the favourite, his father made an ornate robe for him. Now Joseph lacked sensitivity and strutted about in front of his brothers, parading his new robe. If you were to ask Joseph who he was at that time, he might have answered, '*I am my father's favourite.*' His identity lay in his relationship with his father.

Joseph then had dreams about the future and he explained the dreams to his brothers. If you were to ask Joseph who he was at that time, he might have answered, '*I am an interpreter of dreams.*' His identity lay in his capability (or gifting).

Many of us go through a similar process in our own lives. For example, we define ourselves by our relationships, our capabilities, our roles in society or in our work. It is this last category I'd like us to explore a little further.

A lady at a dinner party asked the man sitting beside her, '*Tell me something about who you are without reference to your job or possessions.*' The man was stumped and unable to reply. The point being that for many of us we define ourselves by our roles in the workplace.

I have heard that statistically, in the West, the two most dangerous years of our lives are our birth year and the year of our retirement. The first year is understandable because of potential complications over childbirth. The second is more puzzling. Could it be that the loss of identity that often accompanies retirement causes stress, anxiety, fear and loss of purpose?

Work can offer a sense of identity but for Christians, it is not meant to be that way. Instead, we are designed to be *secure in our identity* and for our workplace endeavours to flow from that secure place. Practically this might mean that we ask ourselves at the start of each working day, '*Who am I before God?*' and to do this without reference to our work. The simple act of reading and recalling relevant Scriptures to this effect can be useful.[7]

David Seamands suggests that identity formed by an incorrect self-image is Satan's deadliest weapon. He writes:

Satan's greatest psychological weapon is a gut-level feeling of inferiority, inadequacy and low self-worth and this weapon paralyses potential, destroys dreams, ruins relationships and sabotages Christian service.[8]

If identity secured through our work is a frail foundation, what is a stronger and enduring eternal source of identity? As Christians we

---

7. For example: Isaiah 43:4-5; 1 John 3:1; 1 John 2:14-15; Colossians 3:12; 2 Corinthians 3:5.
8. Seamands, David, p. 58, *Healing for Damaged Emotions*. Copyright © 1981, 2015 by David A. Seamands. Used by permission of David C. Cook. May not be further reproduced. All rights reserved.

have three legitimate sources of identity: who we are, what we cost, what we can become. We will take these in turn.

Who we are: Every living person on the earth has been created in the image of God. We each bear the hallmark of God's creative hand on us. We were created by God; all peoples, all nations. In recent history we have seen genocidal wars fought against particular races (the Tutsi people during the Rwanda civil war of 1994, for instance). In many cases this has been accompanied by an attempt to diminish the humanity of the target race. Opponents are seen as less than human and therefore can be exterminated without trouble to conscience, a point argued by David Livingstone Smith in his book *Less Than Human*.[9]

These are extreme examples involving matters of life and death but the enemy (the devil, or Satan) uses this same tactic – that of diminishing the image of God within us – in all walks of life, including the workplace.

So, when you go into work, walk with dignity. This dignity is based on the fact that you have been created in the image of God. Treat others with that same dignity and respect, *irrespective of whether you think their behaviour warrants it*. I guarantee, if you walk like this, even for a day, you will see the difference. It is counter cultural – and you will release significant blessing but you will inevitably face opposition as you pursue it.

---

9. Livingstone Smith, David, *Less than Human: Why We Demean, Enslave and Exterminate Others* (St Martin's Press, 2011).

What we cost: A further source of identity for Christians concerns what we cost, or the price Jesus paid for each of us on the cross.

> *You know that it was not with perishable things such as silver or gold that you were redeemed from the empty way of life handed down to you from your ancestors, but with the precious blood of Christ, a lamb without blemish or defect.* (1 Peter 1:18-19)

The cost was infinite and points to the infinite worth God ascribes to each one of us.

The third source of our worth is **what we can become**. This is not so much about the development of our character whilst here on earth but about what we will become in Christ. One day we will see him face to face and on that day we will be like him. That is the source of our identity and it is unshakeable for it cannot be impacted by our successes or failures.

The writer to the Hebrews talks of a similar certainty in the following words:

> *Since we are receiving a kingdom that cannot be shaken, let us be thankful, and so worship God acceptably with reverence and awe.* (Hebrews 12:28)

This leaves us with a daily choice. Will we choose to draw our identity from sources that God has given, or will we try to find our identity in our own efforts, and particularly through our work endeavours?

In practice we might want to do the following:

i. Offer our daily work to God as an act of service, maybe through a prayer. Simply, this could be expressed as: '*Lord, receive my work today as an act of worship.*' Include an item of thanksgiving.

We may want to add a confession for when we have failed in our worship the preceding day.

ii. Ask the Lord for guidance and help in our work: '*Lord, guide and give wisdom today in the decisions I make and my interactions with others.*' The more specific we can be the better.

iii. Ask the Lord if there is anything else he wants to draw our attention to: '*Lord, is there anything you want to say to me about my day?*' And then we pause and listen.

3.6 Summary

In summary, we have established that:

❖ Humankind searches for purpose in our places of work but this is often elusive because ultimately our souls will only find rest in relationship with the eternal God. Work is an inadequate substitute.

❖ The search for identity in our work is a cul-de-sac. Our identity needs to be placed securely in God and not in our own endeavours.

❖ The striving for purpose and inherent frustration in Creation can have the effect of leading us towards a deeper encounter with God, if we are prepared to reflect on it.

❖ Humankind looks for meaning in work but the scriptural position is the other way round; we are designed to bring meaning to our work.

❖ Work offered to God will in some sense endure beyond this life. This calls for faith and trust, recognising that in some situations, we may see fruit from our labour only in the life to come.

4 Enemy's purpose

As well as God having purpose for our workplaces, it may surprise us to understand that the enemy also has a purpose. His purpose is diametrically opposite to that of God and is motivated by a lust for power and a hatred for God and all in Creation. We will explore the enemy's purpose to ensure that we are not *'unaware of his schemes'* (2 Corinthians 2:11) and that we can stand in faith against his activity.

4.1 The enemy wants to disrupt

The enemy creates discord in the workplace, including pursuit of selfish ambition and discriminatory practices. He is not so much against work but he hates God, he hates all humankind and since what goes on in the workplace matters to God, the enemy will do all he can to disrupt God's plans in the workplace.

Disruption in our places of work often is the result of unseen spiritual influences

So what are the characteristics of the enemy's purpose? Scripture tells us that he cares nothing for God's people.

The thief comes only to steal and kill and destroy; I have come that they may have life, and have it to the full. (John 10:10)

Secondly, the enemy sows deceit, immorality and lies throughout our places of work, distorting the truth where he can. Jesus said to the Pharisees:

You belong to your father, the devil, and you want to carry out your father's desires. He was a murderer from the beginning, not holding to the truth, for there is no truth in him. When he lies, he speaks his native language, for he is a liar and the father of lies. (John 8:44)

For example, I have known of countless marital affairs conducted in the place of work; some covert, others overt. The effects are manifestly disruptive in the lives of those affected, bringing misery and pain.

Thirdly, he attacks Christians in their places of work; specifically with discouragements, accusations and threats.

The great dragon was hurled down – that ancient snake called the devil, or Satan, who leads the whole world astray. He was hurled to the earth, and his angels with him. Then I heard a loud voice in heaven say: 'Now have come the salvation and the power and the kingdom of our God, and the authority of his Messiah. For the accuser of our brothers and sisters, who accuses them before our God day and night, has been hurled down.' (Revelation 12:9-10)

On some occasions I have been on the receiving end of unjust accusations in the workplace. Those accusations have usually stung and it has taken discussion with friends and family to gain other perspectives and bring healing.

It is worth pausing for a moment to ask ourselves what is the enemy's end-purpose in such a strategy? We can see his tactical manoeuvres described above of discord, deceit and discouragements, but what are his real objectives? Let me name three. He wants access to humankind, he wants worship and he wants to cause division.

Firstly, he wants access to humankind in order to gain authority to rule. God gave Adam authority to rule over all Creation in the Garden of Eden and when Adam sinned, this authority was relinquished to the enemy. Jesus reclaimed that authority for us by the cancellation of our sin debt. The enemy continues to want access to humankind and he obtains this whenever we sin or live in rebellion against God. But his end-game is a desire to rule and humankind is the means of obtaining that authority to rule.

The enemy wants to rule in our workplaces too and he does this by influencing people's lives so that sinful practice abounds. Our role as Christians is to lay hold of the authority given to us in Christ and to live obedient lives in our places of work.

Secondly, he wants worship and to draw attention and worship away from God. The enemy cares less about *how* this is accomplished and will use whatever means he can to influence people to worship man-made things, rather than the Creator. These man-made things can include work itself, possessions, money and relationships. In fact, whenever our primary focus (and therefore worship) is away from God, the enemy is satisfied.

Our role personally, therefore, is to make sure that God is central to our lives and that we do not allow other dreams and desires to take God's place.

Finally, the enemy wants to divide humankind from God, others, themselves and their environment.

Wherever in our workplace the enemy is active, chaos and discord are the result

The core of this intention is to spoil what God has created and to deter humankind from establishing a right relationship with God, with others and with ourselves.

4.2 His work is targeted and temporal

In contrast to God's work, which is eternal and expansive, the enemy's work is temporal and targeted. Jesus had undergone his baptism where his heavenly Father affirmed him as his Son.

This is my Son, whom I love; with him I am well pleased. (Matthew 3:17)

Jesus was then led into the desert where Satan tempted him with various allurements. Jesus used both Scripture and what he knew about the character of the Father to defend his position against these attacks. We need to do the same – we will face temptation in the workplace, the question is how we will respond.

After the threefold temptation recorded in Luke 4, the gospel records:

When the devil had finished all this tempting, he left him until an opportune time. (Luke 4:13)

Satan will overstate his power and influence. Let us make no mistake, he is a powerful enemy but the one who is within us is greater still. When Satan had finished his tempting of Jesus, he left him till a later point in Jesus's ministry.

> **Let us note the example of Jesus and not underestimate the value of a regular intake of God's word by reading, studying, hearing, memorising and meditating on Scripture. When we put in the 'spade work' of regularly reading God's word, we will be in a much better position to weather the storms of our working life.**

In our places of work, Satan is already active but his domain is limited and will eventually be overthrown. Our heavenly Father, on the other hand, is active *all the time*. He never slumbers nor sleeps, and he is always at work on our behalf. Jesus said of the Father:

My Father is always at his work to this very day, and I too am working. (John 5:17)

What is the significance for us in our workplaces? We need to make sure our spiritual radar is always on alert. Our enemy is likened to a roaring lion, looking for someone to devour. He is on the prowl and the apostle Paul urges us to not be unaware of his schemes (2 Corinthians 2:11). We need, therefore, to be aware of his activity (which we know is temporal and limited) and be on our guard against it.

Furthermore, we can have confidence that where we work for God's purpose, we are on the winning side. We will face workplace setbacks, discouragements and disappointments, but we know that these will be only temporal.

4.3 Sacred-secular division is part of the enemy's strategy

There is one particular aspect of the enemy's strategy that I want to address in relation to work. It is the sacred-secular divide.

In my early years as a Christian I was brought up on a hierarchy of priorities. God was first, family came second, work third, church fourth and social activities fifth. These, I believed, had some scriptural backing. You might, however, believe differently and would want to move these around into a different order entirely.

It can be said that *'if God is first, there isn't a second'*. In other words, everything we do needs to flow out of the single and only priority for our lives: to glorify God. Mark Greene argued a similar idea, suggesting that life can't be neatly divided up into segments, like the segments of an orange. He likened life to a 'peach',[10] seamless all the way through, having one consistency.

---

10. Greene, Mark, *The Great Divide* (LICC, 2013), p. 10.

Before we look at the implications of this for our work, I want to explore the origins of this thinking. At the time of Christ, the Greeks believed that all matter was essentially evil; it was to be despised and had nothing to do with the soul or spiritual matters. This led to first-century Gnostic teaching which further argued that if matter is non-spiritual, then so are our bodies. If our bodies are not spiritual, then anything we do in our bodies will not taint our souls.

Today we may still see evidence of this error in our churches. Take some of the terms that are prevalent. It might be argued that a worker employed by the church is engaged in *'full-time ministry'*. This is not always an accurate descriptor since it can imply a sacred-secular divide. Our circumstances will vary; our education and gifting also, but in a real sense, we are *all* involved in full-time ministry. There are no exceptions. We may be only using the term as shorthand to mean 'paid worker involved in local church-related activity'. However, it is also useful to recognise how such terms can not only be *descriptive* but *formative* in influencing how we see the world around us.

Or take the term 'Christian'. This word is used in Scripture three times[11] and each time the word is a noun; a word that denotes a person (or thing). The word is never used in Scripture as an adjective (i.e. a word describing a noun) and yet this practice is commonplace today. For instance, the term is used to describe Christian holidays, Christian books, music, plays, art and businesses. Much of this usage is shorthand but it is worth being aware where this is the case and recognising how this shorthand might influence our thinking with regards a sacred-secular divide. For example, when we talk about going on a Christian holiday, what we mean is that it is a holiday organised by Christians (noun), for Christians (noun) and that we

---

11. Acts 26:28, 1 Peter 4:16 and Acts 11:26.

have the expectation that it is run according to biblical principles. We could infer that the Christian holiday is somehow separate from and different from a non-Christian holiday where the above factors are not in place. It then is a short step to begin to believe that the Christian holiday is 'sanctified', is of God and of interest to God's purpose whilst the 'non-Christian holiday' consequentially lies *outside* his domain and interest. This of course is inaccurate and erroneous. A holiday run by an organisation that has no Christian employees and is not identifiably designed along biblical principles can nevertheless be beneficial to us and constructive in our fulfilling God's purpose in our lives. The same can also be said of music, art and literature. Furthermore, by labelling an area of activity as Christian, we may uncritically accept all elements of the activity as being consistent with Scripture, whereas in fact this may not be the case. This thinking can easily impact how we see our workplace too.

Finally, consider the spiritual gifts highlighted in 1 Corinthians 11, applicable to today. How many of us see them as applicable in the marketplace? Do we see church buildings as sacred and the marketplace as secular? If we do, it would naturally follow that the 'sacred' is more important to God than the 'secular'.

We have, therefore, the sacred world (consisting of prayer, spiritual gifts, sacraments, acts of charity, worship, etc.) and we have the secular world (consisting of commerce and the working world). These worlds are seen as separate and divided. But what if no such division exists in the mind of God? I would like to suggest four reasons why there is no such division.

Firstly, it is inconsistent with New Testament teaching. The apostle Paul commanded,

Whatever you do, work at it with all your heart, as working for the Lord, not for human masters. (Colossians 3:23)

There is no hierarchy listed in this teaching; and no separation of a sacred world from a secular world. The word is, "whatever". Whatever we do needs to be offered as an act of service and in submission to His will.

Secondly, it leads to spiritual blindness. If we separate our worlds into two, then it becomes easier to live godly lives in one sphere (the one God cares about) whilst living out completely godless values in the other sphere. This, I believe, is why Christians can find themselves working in a manner inconsistent with biblical teaching. Compartmentalised lives often lead to godlessness, because the yeast of the Word is not being permitted to permeate the *whole* of the dough evenly. Jesus said,

The kingdom of heaven is like yeast that a woman took and mixed into about thirty kilograms of flour until it worked all through the dough. (Matthew 13:33)

This is a lot of dough to work through! The point to note is that it is one lump of dough, not two. There is no sacred world and secular world. There is just one 'world'.

Thirdly, the fruit of the sacred-secular divide is restlessness, disillusionment and disengagement. If we live compartmentalised lives then we will become restless as we seek to live out our lives as Christians. Inevitably, much of our lives will be seen as existing outside the 'sacred' sphere. Our Sunday sermons will have little impact on our working lives because they will be perceived to be of little relevance to the pressures and decisions that need to be made in the workplace. Restlessness is the result.

Sherman and Hendricks add one further impact of the sacred-secular divide:

It destroys your dignity as a worker. If sixty per cent or more of your life doesn't count to God, then you don't count to God.[12]

They add that our work then ceases to have value and we start to see ourselves as second-class citizens in God's kingdom.

Eventually, when the church seems less relevant to our working lives, many grow disillusioned and disengage from their faith altogether. We need respectfully to question and challenge the sacred-secular divide wherever it is manifest.

A person subscribing to a belief in the sacred-secular divide will show some identifiable characteristics. Their primary focus and thinking will be centred on activities within the church environment. Spiritual gifts are seen as appropriate primarily for 'sacred' ends and not 'secular' ones.

Fourthly then, the sacred-secular divide was not modelled in the life of Jesus. Jesus did his miracles often in 'secular settings'. Consider the miraculous catch of fish where Jesus said:

'Put out into deep water, and let down the nets for a catch.' Simon answered, 'Master, we've worked hard all night and haven't caught anything. But because you say so, I will let down the nets.' When they had done so, they caught such a large number of fish that their nets began to break. So they signalled to their partners

---

12. Some content taken from *Your Work Matters to God*, pp. 21, by Doug Sherman and William Hendricks. Copyright © 1987. Used by permission of NavPress, represented by Tyndale House Publishers, a Division of Tyndale House Ministries. All rights reserved.

in the other boat to come and help them, and they came and filled both boats so full that they began to sink. (Luke 5:4-7)

This was a miracle conducted from *within* a boat; the working world of Simon Peter.

> Many of the miracles of Jesus were conducted not in the synagogue (a place considered to be 'sacred') but in the marketplace or the home.

I wonder what our workplaces would look like if we allowed Jesus to teach us from the boat and to perform miraculous acts in that domain. Or consider the miracle of the four-drachma coin. Jesus said:

'What do you think, Simon?' he asked. 'From whom do the kings of the earth collect duty and taxes – from their own children or from others?' 'From others,' Peter answered. 'Then the children are exempt,' Jesus said to him. 'But so that we may not cause offence, go to the lake and throw out your line. Take the first fish you catch; open its mouth and you will find a four-drachma coin. Take it and give it to them for my tax and yours.' (Matthew 17:25-27)

Jesus conducted a miracle not for a 'sacred' purpose but to meet the tax requirements of a 'secular' authority.

So, if for the reasons above, the sacred-secular divide does not exist, what is the enemy's purpose in its creation? I believe the enemy uses the perceived divide to greatly diminish the impact of the

Holy Spirit in our lives. If a large proportion of our waking hours is in a world that is little impacted by our Christian faith (i.e. the 'secular' world), then the enemy has won his cause. If, conversely, we recognise that there is no such divide and open up the *whole* of our lives to the influence of the Holy Spirit, then there is so much greater potential for transformation of our world. God also promises to reward such openness:

> *Whatever you do, work at it with all your heart, as working for the Lord, not for human masters, since you know that you will receive an inheritance from the Lord as a reward.* (Colossians 3:23-24)

How is this accomplished in practice? I would like to offer four suggestions.

Firstly, pray about the 'everyday'. Pray whilst shopping, planning, gardening, playing sports, resting and watching films at the cinema. Develop a conversational style of worship that allows God to speak into your entire world.

Secondly, be open with God about your dreams and ambitions, however 'unspiritual' you think them to be. The psalmist says,

> *Take delight in the LORD, and he will give you the desires of your heart.* (Psalm 37:4)

Squadron Leader Dick Bell had an ambition to drive a hovercraft. He submitted the desire to God and eventually led an expedition to bring primary health care to remote people groups along the Yangtze river. How did he do this? He served by hovercraft.[13]

---

13. This story is recounted in Bell, Dick, *To the Source of the Yangtze* (Hodder & Stoughton, 1991).

When we surrender our personal ambitions to God, God takes note!

Thirdly, develop prayerful rhythms in life that invite participation with God. Celtic Christianity modelled this kind of expression, with early prayers including ones about milking cows, digging peat and making cheese!

Lastly, re-assess how you engage with worship in church settings. Sam and Sara Hargreaves cover this in *Whole Life Worship*:

> *Church worship plays a decisive role in transforming congregations into whole-life disciples. There is the potential that each person can be refreshed, inspired, empowered and sent out to make a difference wherever he or she happens to be.*[14]

For those within the congregation, this can be a matter of 'bringing to our corporate worship our busy week' and allowing God to speak into these situations.

---

14. Hargreaves, Sam and Sara, *Whole Life Worship*, p. 4. Copyright © 2017, used by permission of IVP.

4.4 Summary

In summary, let us note:

❖ The enemy also has a purpose in our places of work; sowing lies, accusations, deceit and disruption.

❖ His work is temporal and targeted. This is in contrast to the work of God which is universal and eternal.

❖ In history, a significant tactic of the enemy has been to instil in the church a false belief in a sacred-secular divide.

❖ The teaching of Scripture and the model of Jesus show us that no such divide exists in the mind of God. He is active and interested in *all* of Creation.

5 Application and prayer

Let us consider what we can do in response to the issues we have explored. What, for instance, do we believe God is saying to us and how do we need to act accordingly? This section contains a few suggestions.

5.1 Recognise that we each have a daily choice

When it comes to work's purpose we each have a daily choice. Either we work for God and to serve the needs of others or we work for ourselves. There are no alternatives available to us – and we must choose between these two on a daily basis.

David was a young man in his first job who asked me for advice about a career decision. He was in a job that he did not enjoy and he wanted to change career (to become a human resources manager). He was studying to gain professional qualifications to that end. But he had an important question. Was his desire to work in human resources from God or was it his own selfish ambition driving his desire? Or in other words, was he fulfilling God's purpose or his own?

In one sense, the very fact that he was asking the question might suggest that selfish ambition was not a problem. Philippians 2:3-4 reminds us:

Do nothing out of selfish ambition or vain conceit. Rather, in humility value others above yourselves, not looking to your own interests but each of you to the interests of the others.

I could see the passion and excitement in David's face as he described his desire to follow a new career path. I believe that this desire wonderfully aligned with God's purpose. His passion stemmed from a desire both to use his gifts and interests and to serve others. When we give these desires to God, he can transform our offerings, our motivations and richly bless our endeavours.

And so it is a good question to ask ourselves and to ask regularly. Are we working for God's purpose or our own? If the answer is the latter, then we need to ask God's forgiveness and then offer our work afresh for his purpose. God is gracious and will transform our lowly efforts and bless them.

5.2 Make use of crafted prayers

Graham Cooke, in his book *Crafted Prayer*, describes an approach to prayer that I believe can greatly help us in many walks of life, including our working world. Summarised here, his approach includes the following steps:

i.   **Step 1: Listen to God.** Take time to listen to God with pen and notebook at hand. Listen undistracted for pictures, words, Scriptures, songs, impressions and the like. Ask God to speak into your work situation and to bring to mind whatever he wants with regards to your work.

ii. **Step 2: Craft a prayer.** Having captured these thoughts on paper, begin to craft a written prayer that pulls together the threads of what you believe God has said to you by his Holy Spirit.

iii. **Step 3: Refine the prayer.** Once the prayer is complete, ask God about it. *Lord, is there anything else you want to say?* Refine the prayer and do not be afraid to make changes until each phrase and thought reflects well what you believe God is saying about your work. It may include attitudes he wants you to keep in mind. It may include daily challenges you face and your response to them.

iv. **Step 4: Use the prayer in daily worship over an extended period of time.**

If this helps, I commend this approach to you with regard to your working life and to help you walk in God's purpose. To date, I have written two crafted prayers: one for members of my family and the other for my home and the usage to which it is put. Work is next on the list!

5.3 Prayer

Lord, I believe you have a purpose for my work.

I confess that I have not always sought your purpose and at times have followed my own ambitions and agenda.

There are occasions, too, when I have not grasped the truth you have declared over humankind and instead, I have sought to establish my identity through the work that I do.

For this I ask for your forgiveness.

I believe that I am your workmanship, created in Jesus to do good works which you have prepared in advance for me to do. I believe that you have called me to bear your image in my work.

May I faithfully bear your image as I go about my work. And where, Lord, I search for meaning, I commit that desire to you.

You know the desires of our hearts, the desire to see our efforts rewarded, the desire for encouragement: a 'well done, good and faithful servant'.

Lord, be pleased with all I offer of my work.

Lord, I give you thanks that in your hands, you can take our work offerings and use them for eternal purposes. Take my work and use it how you will.

Help me to partner with you as I go about my daily work. Amen.

Chapter Two

Presence of God in the Workplace

I will ask the Father, and he will give you another advocate to help
you and be with you for ever – the Spirit of truth.
(John 14:16)

1 Introduction

We started with God's purpose for our work. I want now to look at
his presence in our place of work. The knowledge and assurance of
his presence resources us to live the Christian life better when faced
with challenges that inevitably arise. We will look at the presence of
the Father, Son and Holy Spirit.

2 Presence of the Father

I am convinced that God wants us to be more aware of his presence
in our workplaces, to invite and welcome his manifest presence
there. I've known of Christians praying as they enter their physical
buildings, *'Lord, I welcome your presence here. I acknowledge that you*
are sovereign over this place and today I choose to walk with you as I
go about my work.' That's a good place to start.

We can welcome God's presence as we enter our places of work

2.1 The presence of the Father is available to those who ask

Moses met Father God on the mountain and after receiving the commands of God, the Lord instructed him to leave to explore and take the land of Canaan.

> *Go up to the land flowing with milk and honey. But I will not go with you, because you are a stiff-necked people and I might destroy you on the way. (Exodus 33:3)*

These are hardly encouraging words. Indeed the people responded in their distress by a period of mourning. But before we get to the response of Moses, it is worth us reflecting a moment on the natural consequences of our fallen nature when it comes to our places of work. Unless it is for the grace and favour of God given to us as his followers, we would have no assurance of the presence of God in our workplaces. His manifest presence there is not a right but a gift of his grace. It cannot be demanded. Instead, it needs to be asked for and received with gratitude. As believers, the Holy Spirit is always with us but the presence of God is manifest in our environment by prayerful invitation.

After seeing a vision of the face of God, Moses prays,

> *If you are pleased with me, teach me your ways so I may know you and continue to find favour with you. Remember that this nation is your people. The* LORD *replied, 'My Presence will go with you, and I will give you rest.' Then Moses said to him, 'If your Presence does not go with us, do not send us up from here. How will anyone know that you are pleased with me and with your people unless you go with us? What else will distinguish me and your people from all the other people on the face of the earth?' And the* LORD *said to Moses, 'I will do the very thing you have asked, because I am pleased with you and I know you by name.'* (Exodus 33:13-17)

Moses knew that the task ahead was momentous and he felt acutely the additional burden of leading over one million men, women and children to occupy a land and to establish a nation in Canaan. So he prayed for God's presence with him and God assured him that his prayers were answered.

2.2 Desperation and realising the presence

Can you hear the anguish in Moses's voice as you read this text? His challenge was insurmountable. He was desperate for the presence of the Father with him to accomplish his task. The stronger our desperation for his manifest presence, the stronger will be our *awareness* of his presence. If we are half-hearted or indifferent to the presence of God in our workplaces, we will probably not notice if he is there or not. His presence does not depend on our desire, but our appreciation of his presence does.

It is not just the enormity of the task ahead for which we need the assurance of his presence. We need that same assurance whenever we fail to exhibit the fruit of the Spirit in our workplaces. When we fail, we need to know that we can ask God's forgiveness and be confident of his continued presence despite our stumbling. As the psalmist put it:

The LORD makes firm the steps of the one who delights in him ... though he may stumble, he will not fall, for the LORD upholds him with his hand. (Psalm 37:23, 24)

Let us then ask ourselves, are we assured of the presence of the Father with us in our places of work? At the end of this chapter, there is a prayer to ask God for such assurance.

2.3 What do we mean by manifest presence?

However, before we proceed, we have not explained what is meant by God's 'manifest presence'. Surely God is everywhere all the time and we do not need to invite his presence at all into our places of work? As theologians express it, God is transcendent. But God is also manifest or immanent in our broken world. He is both transcendent and immanent. He presides over all of Creation and also visits us with interventions and miracles in our places of work.

So, when we pray for God's manifest presence, we are asking for daily interventions and miracles in our workplaces. When we ask, we would do well to remember that God is also transcendent. He is not *'at our beck and call'*; a God of our own making to fulfil our personal work objectives. Yet he invites us to call on him for help as it relates to our workplaces. There is, therefore, a creative tension for us to observe; *both* of God's transcendence and immanence, or manifest presence.

2.4 Sometimes we wrestle against the presence

Before we look further at the presence of the Godhead in the workplace, I want to consider how we as Christians might respond to the Father's presence. For Moses, the presence of the Father was a necessity.

> *If your Presence does not go with us, do not send us up from here.* (Exodus 33:15)

For us, we might not always, at all times, believe this is the case. We may find the prospect of the Father's presence *uncomfortable*.

One of the reasons that some of us struggle to welcome the Father's presence may lie in our own relationship with our earthly father. If we have had an unfavourable experience with our earthly father, this can affect our view of Father God and in turn impact how we see God at work within our workplace context. This area is outside the scope of this book. However, there are many resources available to help explore the subject further.

Jesus said:

Which of you, if your son asks for bread, will give him a stone? Or if he asks for a fish, will give him a snake? If you, then, though you are evil, know how to give good gifts to your children, how much more will your Father in heaven give good gifts to those who ask him! (Matthew 7:9-11)

Jesus encouraged his disciples to look beyond their earthly parents and to draw *contrasts* in order to see the true nature of our heavenly Father. We can do the same. If your earthly father was not generous, consider then the generosity of God and ask him to reveal by his Spirit what that looks like – even in our places of work. Reflect on it and walk in the opposite spirit – thank God for his generosity to you and look for opportunities to demonstrate the generosity of the Father to our work colleagues.

Before we move on, there is a further aspect of our childhood experiences that I want to explore. We can at times transfer *images* of our earthy father onto our relationship with God. We can also inherit *childhood values* that do not serve us well in the workplace. Let me share two examples.

Throughout most of my teenage years I lived in fear both in my school environment and in my neighbourhood. I carried this same fear into the workplace when it came to relating to those in authority over me. At work I shied away from meaningful interaction with department heads, directors and anyone in managerial roles. In a real sense, my *work was hindered* due to my fear of those in authority.

Or take Madeline who was brought up in a home where intellect, reasoning and 'thinking' where highly valued and where feelings were despised and seldom acknowledged. When Madeline in her adult life was asked by her boss how she felt about a business change, she responded with, *"I'm not paid to feel, I'm only paid to think."* Madeline since has said that such a belief had its downsides in her workplace. In her own words:

> *Thinking and reason were high-value currency in my early years. I lived by them and valued them. I naturally carried these values over into my place of work. As a Christian I began to see the downsides of my childhood values – and began to question them. The main difference I noticed as I explored the value of feelings was an improvement in my ability to empathise with fellow colleagues and team members.*

These examples show how, unchecked, our childhood experiences can adversely influence our working lives – and when questioned and addressed can lead to a richer Christian expression in the workplace.

2.5 Presence is not just for our comfort

Before we move on to the presence of Jesus in our workplaces I want us to think further about 'comfort'. We might seek the presence of God in our workplaces because we are facing work challenges that cause us anxiety and concern. We long for the personal comfort of his presence. This is entirely natural and much of Scripture promises this comfort as we call on him.

> *I sought the LORD and he answered me; he delivered me from all my fears.* (Psalm 34:4)

But there is another aspect to his presence. His presence can bring disruption and challenge to our schools, colleges, hospitals, prisons and corporations.

> When we invite his presence into our places of work; let us be aware that in some cases this will mean changes will need to happen. These changes will always be for the better, but they are changes nonetheless and sometimes will be personally challenging.

On one occasion I found that the work of my team was consistently being evaluated and challenged by that of another team elsewhere within the business. The process was wearing and I could see that mistrust, suspicion and possibly jealously lay at its heart. I prayed over a few weeks concerning the matter and felt the Lord telling me to believe the best of others and to actively demonstrate trust, even though everything within me cried out otherwise. I met with the team leader and had an open and honest conversation about my concerns. Gradually, a greater level of trust was built between the teams and we identified that there were wider incentives and drivers outside of our teams that were not bringing collaborative working. The underlying cause began to become clearer. God brought change for the better whilst I found the process of realising that change to be challenging.

In our workplaces we might experience an element of routine. Routines can be good, but ruts are not. The presence of God in our places of work will transform our experience of work to become more meaningful and fruitful. Either way, God's presence in our places of work is not just for our comfort. His presence is for his purpose, not ours.

2.6 Presence is needed when we face dark places

There will be times when we need the Father's presence in our dark times. On one occasion, I had been working for an organisation for a number of years and had an increasing sense that my time of employment was drawing to a close. This was not my preferred option. Others within my department had been made redundant and I saw the negative impact this had not only on those who left but those who remained within the business. Working relationships became edgy, sometimes toxic. After a period of six months, it became clear that my work was no longer required. I can hardly describe the sense of pain and rejection I felt; hurt mixed with anger.

For a period of two years after, I first learned how to forgive those who had hurt me, praying God's blessing on their lives and releasing them in forgiveness. I sought to look for any redeeming aspect of the redundancy, and there were some. Over that time I stopped my Bible reading plan and spent all my devotions in the Psalms. This was a tremendous comfort and strength to me as I experienced the presence of the Father in my 'dark place'.

Where can I go from your Spirit? Where can I flee from your presence? If I go up to the heavens, you are there; if I make my bed in the depths, you are there. If I rise on the wings of the dawn, if I settle on the far side of the sea, even there your hand will guide me, your right hand will hold me fast. (Psalm 139:7-10)

As well as finding points of identification in the Psalms, there were promises too that became rich in meaning and a source of great comfort. Through the redundancy process I felt out of my depth, outnumbered and outgunned. The Father spoke words of comfort to me:

He reached down from on high and took hold of me; he drew me out of deep waters. He rescued me from my powerful enemy, from my foes, who were too strong for me. They confronted me in the day of my disaster, but the LORD was my support. He brought me out into a spacious place; he rescued me because he delighted in me. (Psalm 18:16-19)

At the time I could only feel the pain but the Father promised his presence with me and that he would bring me out from darkness into a 'spacious place'. This was a promise that I clung to and that helped sustain me throughout the process. The act of listening to God throughout that time served to remind me that I didn't need to accept all that was said over me by others and in some cases it was right and proper to *'refute every tongue that accuses you'* (Isaiah 54:17).

I also learned more of the Father's loving provision for us as a family – and in this process the fear of not having sufficient started to subside as I began to trust him for our needs.

2.7 Not a fearful presence

The fear of the Lord is a common theme in the Old Testament. In the New Testament, reference is made to the sense of awe experienced by worshippers of the Old Covenant. But under the New Covenant, there is a difference. The writer to the book of Hebrews explains:

You have not come to a mountain that can be touched and that is burning with fire; to darkness, gloom and storm; to a trumpet blast or to such a voice speaking words that those who heard it begged that no further word be spoken to them, because they could not bear what was commanded: 'If even an animal touches the mountain, it must be stoned to death.' The sight was so terrifying that Moses said, 'I am trembling with fear.' But you have come to Mount Zion, to the city of the living God, the heavenly Jerusalem. You have come to thousands upon thousands of angels in joyful assembly. (Hebrews 12:18-22)

The sense of awe in the presence of God remains a good thing for us as Christians but now we are encouraged to approach God's throne (to enjoy his presence) with boldness. We have moved from 'trembling fear' to 'joyful assembly'.

> **Unless we are assured of God's complete acceptance of us and his invitation to enjoy his presence, we will remain fearful. This applies equally to our awareness of his presence in the workplace. God is no longer remote, distant and inaccessible but near, approachable and reachable.**

We now have his law written on our hearts and God has promised to do an internal work in our hearts to move us to loving obedience:

I will make an everlasting covenant with them: I will never stop doing good to them, and I will inspire them to fear me, so that they will never turn away from me. (Jeremiah 32:40)

Given this New Covenant, we are no longer to tremble with fear at his presence. As a consequence, we can welcome his presence in our places of work with confidence and without fear. This lack of *fear in his presence* is not to be confused with a *fear of God* – in that we hold him with great honour, awe and deeply held respect for his ways.

2.8 Summary

In summary, we note the following:

❖ God invites us to welcome his manifest presence into our places of work. Just as Moses in desperation called to be assured of God's presence, so we too are urged to seek his presence in all we do.

❖ Our approach to God as heavenly Father will, in part, be shaped by our own experiences with our human father. God can redeem any parental model we have experienced, if we allow him.

❖ When we seek the Father's presence we need to be mindful that his presence may provoke a reaction from others. This is to be expected, since we are entering a battlefield where kingdoms are in conflict.

❖ In the workplace there will be situations where we need to trust God *in the darkness*. These can be opportunities to grow in faith and love.

❖ The presence of the Father is not a fearful presence. He encourages us to approach his throne of grace boldly and with great joy.

3 Presence of Jesus

The presence of Jesus in our places of work is a promise given to us and that promise applies to all persons of the Godhead: Father, Son and Holy Spirit. We might ask ourselves, '*Why emphasise the different persons of the Godhead at all? Why not just talk about God being present in our places of work? Is that not sufficient? Do we need to separately identify Father, Son and Holy Spirit?'*

Certainly, there is no requirement for us to consider the separate persons of the Godhead in relation to God's presence in our workplaces. But before we dismiss this approach, let us consider the following perspectives.

If we reflect solely on God as Father, we may be more likely to see God as distant from our concerns. He transcends all of Creation but we might struggle to recognise his interest in our daily affairs at work. God *within us*, in the form of the Holy Spirit, helps redress our understanding.

Similarly, if we reflect solely on God in the form of Jesus, we might recognise that he is for us, calls us brothers and sisters and teaches us. But we might find it more difficult to recognise him as all-powerful over our cities, nations and world, although the teaching of Colossians instructs us otherwise.

What we are saying, in summary, is that there are benefits to be had in recognising the presence of all three persons – Father, Son and Holy Spirit – in our places of work. Let us look further at what the presence of Jesus means to us.

3.1 Jesus brought his presence to the workplace

Early on in his teaching ministry[15] Jesus stood by the Lake of Gennesaret whilst the crowds gathered to listen to his words.

He saw at the water's edge two boats, left there by the fishermen, who were washing their nets. He got into one of the boats, the

---

15. As opposed to 'carpentry ministry'.

one belonging to Simon, and asked him to put out a little from shore. Then he sat down and taught the people from the boat. (Luke 5:2-3)

If we are tempted to skip over these verses as solely describing a culture and timeline distant from ours, let us remember what the boat represented to Simon. His boat was his *place of work*, since Simon was a fisherman. The act of stepping into a boat was more than a pragmatic solution to the need to speak to the whole crowd without them pressing in on him. Jesus was, by stepping into the boat, entering into Simon's workplace. It was from there that he spoke to the crowds.

Our Sunday service sermons will sometimes address the specific needs of the challenges we face in our workplaces. However, the challenges we face are unique and we cannot reasonably expect to find answers to all our concerns through sermon and teaching material delivered to a wider audience in our churches on a Sunday morning.

We need to discern, listen and reflect on what we experience *in our places of work* and the knowledge of Christ's presence 'teaching from the boat' is a comfort to us. He will teach us if we are willing to listen. I have found that short prayers in the workplace asking for wisdom, guidance and strength all to be helpful. We can all pray and ask for the Lord's help who will teach us *'from the boat'*.

The greatest learning, however, can come from *reflection* on these experiences. Jesus, from within the boat, stilled the storm and then asked the disciples to reflect on their response: *'Why are you so afraid?'* (Matthew 8:26).

As we call to Jesus in prayer, we will experience his manifest presence. As we reflect on our experience, then we will experience a more lasting impact.

3.2 The promise of Jesus's presence is not conditional upon going somewhere

If the Sea of Gennesaret underlies the implicit promise of the presence of Jesus in our places of work, Matthew's gospel makes his promise explicit. The passage reads:

> *Then the eleven disciples went to Galilee, to the mountain where Jesus had told them to go. When they saw him, they worshipped him; but some doubted. Then Jesus came to them and said, 'All authority in heaven and on earth has been given to me. Therefore go and make disciples of all nations, baptising them in the name of the Father and of the Son and of the Holy Spirit, and teaching them to obey everything I have commanded you. And surely I am with you always, to the very end of the age.'*
> (Matthew 28:16-20)

These are, to many of us, familiar words. They contain the Great Commission, where Jesus instructed the Eleven to make disciples. The command to 'go' given to the Eleven was a command to leave the land of Israel and to teach other nations; to spread the Good News abroad. In the twenty-first century, if we live outside Israel we are those nations. The command to make disciples and teach applies to us where we are living. So for us, the sense of the passage might be 'as you go, make disciples' or 'as you go about your lives and daily work, make disciples'. It is not necessarily a command to cross a sea and move to another country to propagate the Christian message, although I am certainly not discounting that the Holy Spirit is calling many in this way. It is, instead, a command to make disciples *wherever we are*. As we take the presence of Jesus into our workplaces and model our work practices on his character, we will inevitably be introducing others to kingdom values and to the king.

The promise of the presence of Jesus, therefore, is not conditional on us going somewhere, because we are already there. The promise is given as an assurance of his presence to resource us to be salt and light[16] in *every living circumstance*, including our places of work.

> We can be confident of the presence of Jesus in our places of work not only because he demonstrated it in the life of the disciples but because he promised it in the Great Commission.

What difference does it make to know the presence of Jesus with us in our places of work as opposed to the presence of the Father? There is too little space to properly address this question here. But the answer does lie in the nature of the Father and the nature of Jesus, as revealed in Scripture.

3.3 Jesus is a present friend of workers

When we think of the presence of Jesus, we might want to reflect on the fact that Jesus taught his disciples, he walked with them, he showed them how to pray, he lived an example for them to follow, he challenged the values of the world. He showed them how to live in

---

16. Jesus uses this metaphor in the Sermon on the Mount (Matthew 5:13-14).

dependence and trust in the Father, he encouraged them to be bold, he sympathised with them in their weaknesses, he believed in them, he restored them when they suffered setbacks and failure and he loved them. He calls us to rely on and reflect those same characteristics as we go about our work.

When we remind ourselves of those same characteristics – we can experience the reality of the presence of Jesus in our places of work. But this needs to go beyond a cerebral exercise (i.e. reminding ourselves of truths). It needs to be experienced and lived out. I believe we can experience the presence of Jesus by a daily conversation in the tasks of the working day, as we would any friend with whom we want to share our lives and know intimately. God invites us to partner with him. Our conversations can be of seemingly trivial matters or about important decisions that need to be made – but the important thing is that they are authentic and conversational.

3.4 Jesus sympathises with our weaknesses in the workplace

Hebrews 4:15 says of Jesus:

> *For we do not have a high priest who is unable to feel sympathy*
> *for our weaknesses, but we have one who has been tempted in*
> *every way, just as we are – yet he did not sin.*

Jesus sympathises with our weaknesses and frailties in our places of work. We will make mistakes and be responsible for errors of judgement, but we can draw comfort from knowing that Jesus invites us to *'approach God's throne of grace with confidence'* (Hebrews 4:16).

Practically speaking this means that if we err in our places of work, we are not bound under God to atone for those errors – that has already been accomplished for us at the cross. We can continue to approach the throne of grace or, in other words, we can continue to rely on the presence of Jesus to assist us in our places of work. If we ask for forgiveness we will be assured of his love, since *'love covers over a multitude of [wrongs]'* (1 Peter 4:8).

3.5 Summary

❖ Jesus taught the disciples from the boat and this serves as an example to us that he is prepared to step into our world, to teach us about how to live in our places of work.

❖ The promise Jesus gives to his disciples of his presence applies equally today. In the Great Commission, Jesus promised he would be with us and this includes in our work environment.

❖ Jesus faced and overcame human struggles and is able to sympathise with us in our frailties. He invites us to be authentic in our daily conversations with him.

4 Presence of the Spirit

Let us consider the Holy Spirit and his presence with us in our places of work. We will make the distinction between the *presence* of the Holy Spirit in us and the *manifestation* of the Holy Spirit in our places of work.

4.1 Presence of the Spirit is now guaranteed

In the Old Testament, the Holy Spirit was given on occasions to specific people for specific times. For example, the Spirit came upon Samson:

Samson went down to Timnah together with his father and mother. As they approached the vineyards of Timnah, suddenly a young lion came roaring towards him. The Spirit of the LORD *came powerfully upon him so that he tore the lion apart with his bare hands as he might have torn a young goat. But he told neither his father nor his mother what he had done.* (Judges 14:5-6)

The presence of the Holy Spirit was by no means guaranteed or certain, for David wrote after he had sinned against Bathsheba:

Create in me a pure heart, O God, and renew a steadfast spirit within me. Do not cast me from your presence or take your Holy Spirit from me. Restore to me the joy of your salvation and grant me a willing spirit, to sustain me. (Psalm 51:10-12)

In the New Testament, and post Pentecost, the situation is different. Jesus promised:

I will ask the Father, and he will give you another advocate to help you and be with you forever – the Spirit of truth. The world cannot accept him, because it neither sees him nor knows him. But you know him, for he lives with you and will be in you. (John 14:16-17)

As followers of Jesus, the presence of the Holy Spirit is given to us for ever, a deposit guaranteeing our inheritance. He lives within us. As we operate in our places of work, he is with us because he lives within us. His *manifest presence*[17] in the workplace is seen by invitation.

4.2 The Spirit brings fruit and gifts

The fruit of the Holy Spirit are important; not only important but

---

17. A manifest presence is one that is perceived by faith, *sometimes* through the five senses.

essential in our Christian lives if we are to live as God intended. The Holy Spirit also equips us with spiritual gifts, many of which are listed in the New Testament as being relevant and applicable for today. (For a full debate on this point, I recommend Grudem's *Systematic Theology*.[18])

We may belong to a church that acknowledges the gifts of the Holy Spirit and that seeks to encourage church members to exercise those gifts. However, frequently the arena for exercising those gifts is seen as limited to the church setting. In practice, the gifts are equally given for mission and the marketplace. The Holy Spirit does not say, '*We are entering the place of work now, so let's focus on fruit; I don't really do gifts here.*' The Spirit gives gifts to God's people for use *in their places of work.*

Shearer, in his book *The Marketplace Christian*,[19] describes how we might think differently about spiritual gifts in the workplace. For instance, a person with the spiritual gift of discernment might use their gift to work in cyber security, identifying vulnerabilities of computer systems to attack from malevolent sources. Or another with the gift of teaching might use their gift in the IT training department of a large organisation. The list can go on, and Shearer's perspective is useful to cause us to think differently about the application of spiritual gifts we see in Scripture.

Bezalel was the first person named in Scripture that was filled with the Spirit of God. He was an artisan and craftsman. God took his craftsmanship and filled him with wisdom, understanding and

---

18. Grudem, Wayne, *Systematic Theology* (Zondervan Academic, 1994).
19. Shearer, Darren, *The Marketplace Christian: A Practical Guide to Using Your Spiritual Gifts in Business*, Kindle Edition (High Bridge Books, 2015).

knowledge. That same wisdom is available today to those who follow Jesus.

As I write during Covid-19 lockdown, I have been working on an unsolved business problem for two weeks. The numbers have been calculated and the analysis complete. The outcome of the work could influence the business for years to come. But I'm aware that a supernatural breakthrough is required if progress is to be made. Wisdom, knowledge and understanding all have their part in our working lives, but there are times when we come to the end of ourselves and have to ask for God's intervention.

What I have described about spiritual gifts being available in the workplace, could also be said to be true of the ministries listed in the book of Ephesians: apostles, pastors, evangelists, teachers and prophets. Whilst these ministries are given that the church may be built up, there is nothing in Scripture to say that their influence is restricted to church communities. They can operate equally in the marketplace.

What does that look like for us? It means we can pray, just as the apostles did, for the manifest presence of the Holy Spirit, for the release of gifts and miracles in our places of work. Pray for wisdom, knowledge, healing, miracles and prophetic words. Speak in tongues, serve, encourage, give gifts and exercise faith. All these can be done in the context of our places of work.

Sophie had led a small team for just over two years. She was concerned that one of her team members had, over a six-month period, become particularly disruptive in the workplace. One of Sophie's directors had pointed out that a termination of contract was something to be considered. Sophie's initial position was to hold out – hoping and expecting that changes in behaviour would follow.

When no such changes happened and the team morale further deteriorated, Sophie described how she went for a lunchtime walk and prayed over the matter. Then something unusual happened. She had an acute sense that the Lord was saying, *'The matter will be resolved very soon.'* When she got back to her desk she saw a letter of resignation. Having been forewarned by the Lord, Sophie was in a better position to act quickly, accept the resignation and make it effective immediately. Sophie assured her team member as best as she could of the support of the organisation in managing the change, including a payment in excess of his legal entitlement, and wished her team member well for the future. The wider team understood the decision and responded well to the news.

Some may find this application of the gifts of the Spirit to be startling or even concerning. However, let us observe that difficult decisions need to be made within our places of work and I'm convinced that the Lord's help is required for all our work-based decisions. According to Scripture, gifts of the Holy Spirit need to be 'eagerly sought' if we are going to see them manifest (in our places of work). As we seek those gifts, let us not be surprised that the Lord speaks into all our workplace matters, even if we find them to be challenging or uncomfortable.

4.3 Manifest at times

I have made the distinction between the presence of the Holy Spirit (within us at all times) and the manifestation of the Holy Spirit (evidenced in answer to prayer). In Acts, the apostles prayed that God would enable them to speak his word boldly, to heal and perform signs and wonders. It records:

After they prayed, the place where they were meeting was shaken.
And they were all filled with the Holy Spirit and spoke the word
of God boldly. (Acts 4:31)

The manifestation of the Holy Spirit came in answer to prayer. This resulted in not only bold proclamations of the gospel message but in generous giving and a heart for the poor amongst the church of that day.

Whilst we can be assured of the presence of the Holy Spirit in us, we can still pray for his presence to be manifest in our places of work. What will that look like? Certainly it will be different in different circumstances and it will take spiritual discernment to see.

A few years ago I was at a church event (an evening Ball) run by the youth group to raise money for an overseas mission trip. I had invited friends from work along to the event and the evening was about to get into full swing. At this point, my church pastor came over and privately asked me a question. *'What do you see God doing here at this Ball? And what is the enemy doing?'* I was dumbfounded. At that point, the only thoughts in my mind were, *'What's on the menu, are my friends enjoying themselves and where can I get a glass of Chardonnay?'* I did not have an immediate answer for my pastor but as I considered his question I began to see a number of unusual behaviours that might have suggested a disruptive enemy influence.

To see what God is already doing requires discernment but also requires that we take time and practise asking the Father, *'Lord, what are you doing?'* Since the time of the Ball in the example above, I have increasingly asked that question. The question I now ask is, *'Lord, what do you want to draw my attention to here?'* and then wait to see his answer.

The Holy Spirit is active in our places of work already, if we are prepared to look and to ask him to reveal what he is doing.

4.4 The Spirit already there

The Spirit of God is present everywhere. It would be a mistake to think that when we enter our workplaces we bring the Spirit of God with us since he is already there. What we hopefully bring is a life submitted to God's purpose and indwelt by God's Spirit. We have seen this in history where missionaries have visited unreached peoples only to find evidence that God is already at work in some measure in their lives. What the missionary can bring is a fuller revelation of the character of God. The apostle Paul, for instance, to the men of Athens proclaimed:

The very thing you worship – and this is what I am going to proclaim to you. (Acts 17:23)

What are the implications of this for us? We need to tread with humility and recognise that God is already at work wherever we go.

Josh met with a group of Christian men in a pub each week where he said that he was a 'seeker', wanting to know more about the Christian faith. Many hours were spent trying to persuade him of the authenticity and reliability of the gospel accounts, but he did not seem to move in his convictions, describing himself as an agnostic. Fast forward fifteen years and Josh was invited to join a small fellowship group, which met in people's homes. There, Josh still described himself as an agnostic.

On one occasion, he was asked a question by a member of the group: *'Tell us about your spiritual journey, where did it start?'* It was then they learned something new. Josh had felt that God had called him to work in a paid church role. He had applied through the normal channels but his application had been refused, which he took to be 'rejection' by God. The group member then remarked on all he was doing in serving the community, particularly amongst disadvantaged young people. Josh was serving God, just in a different capacity. Josh realised that God still had a call on his life; nothing had changed. He then rededicated his life to following God and the change in his whole demeanour was remarkable, particularly in the small-group setting.

The point of this story is that when we recognise the work that God has *already done,* we are better able to cooperate, or partner with his purpose in others' lives.

4.5 Summary

Let us summarise:

- ❖ In the Old Testament, the Holy Spirit was seen to be given to specific people at specific times for specific tasks. For us as Christians, the Holy Spirit is given to all, for all times and for all circumstances.

- ❖ The Holy Spirit transforms us to become more like Jesus in character, growing in us the fruit of the Spirit. The gifts of the Spirit are for use as much in the marketplace as in the church; they are for use wherever God wills.

- ❖ The Holy Spirit is always present but manifest (in ways we can perceive) at certain times. We can pray for an increase of his manifest presence in our places of work.

- ❖ The Holy Spirit is already present in our workplaces, and at work in others' lives. When we cooperate with what he is doing, greater fruit is often the result.

5 Impact of God's presence

Much of what we have considered so far has centred on knowing and being assured of the presence of God the Father, Son and Holy Spirit in our places of work. We will now look at the impact of God's presence in our workplaces.

5.1 God's presence is designed to have impact

If we are honest, part of us seeks to shut God out. It is almost too uncomfortable to accept the challenge of Jesus to be like salt and light.

Personally, there have been many times when I have asked myself the question, *'How different is my life as a Christian?'* Jesus challenged us:

> *Whoever wants to be my disciple must deny themselves and take up their cross daily and follow me.* (Luke 9:23)

Fortunately, in Jesus, we have someone who is able to sympathise with our weaknesses and who forgives us and restores us when we fall. But let us be honest with ourselves. We love to be appreciated, acknowledged, praised by the world and this kind of 'longing to be loved' has the power to ensnare us unless we recognise and repent of it. Let us instead *'always be prepared'*[20] by being available to the Lord to speak about him to others – and even asking him daily who he would have us speak to.

Furthermore, Jesus invited his disciples to follow him and become fishers of people. That same invitation is open to us today. If we ask him, he will show us how to bear witness in our places of work.

---

20. See 1 Peter 3:15

When I have read of prominent Christian business leaders who have been fined, and in some cases imprisoned, for illegal practices, part of me has wept, wondering how this could happen. Timothy Keller takes this further and suggests that merely asking whether a practice is ethical is not sufficient and that we need to ask more searching questions about the business with which we are engaged.[21]

> Unless we *examine ourselves and practices carefully*, it is too easy to live a life in our workplaces that bears little resemblance to the life of Christ. We need God's help and to be prepared to humble ourselves to ask for it.

We can start with recognising and welcoming the presence of God in our places of work. His presence in our places of work will always have impact.

5.2 God's presence is for God's purpose

His presence is not just for our benefit, it is for his kingdom. Daniel saw the presence of God manifest in a hostile environment and the initial impact was adversarial, but it did serve ultimately to further the kingdom of God on earth.

King Nebuchadnezzar had a dream that unsettled him and he called on Daniel, a follower of God, to interpret it for him. Daniel explained the dream to the king:

---

21. Paraphrased from Keller, Timothy, *Every Good Endeavour: Connecting Your Work to God's Work* (Penguin, 2012) p. 202.

You will be driven away from people and will live with the wild animals; you will eat grass like the ox and be drenched with the dew of heaven. (Daniel 4:25)

The king was not a God-fearing man. He recognised the Spirit of God in Daniel, just as many in our place of work will do of us. Daniel brought a warning to the king:

Your Majesty, be pleased to accept my advice: renounce your sins by doing what is right, and your wickedness by being kind to the oppressed. It may be that then your prosperity will continue. (Daniel 4:27)

But the king did not heed that warning and continued about his daily business.

From time to time we will see setbacks in our places of work and appear to make no ground in advancing God's kingdom on earth. This may be an issue of timing. God is at work and we need only to be patient.

King Nebuchadnezzar sometime later came to a realisation:

I, Nebuchadnezzar, raised my eyes towards heaven, and my sanity was restored. Then I praised the Most High; I honoured and glorified him who lives forever. His dominion is an eternal dominion; his kingdom endures from generation to generation. (Daniel 4:34)

Nebuchadnezzar recognised God's sovereignty over all of Creation.

> The presence of God in Daniel's place of work had impact that he was to see unfold *only over time.* Indeed this presence was not seen until after Daniel had visited the lion's den! It may be the same with us.

5.3 God's presence at the end

We have shown in this chapter an evolution. With Moses, the presence of God was at first uncertain and not guaranteed. It was given to a specific people in response to their obedience under the terms of a covenant. In the life of followers of Jesus, the presence of God in us through the Holy Spirit is certain and guaranteed.

At the end times, God's presence will take on a new reality where he lives among us. The book of Revelation paints a picture:

God's dwelling-place is now among the people, and he will dwell with them. They will be his people, and God himself will be with them and be their God. (Revelation 21:3)

How we see this verse is important since it concerns God's presence among his people. We can either work towards it or work from it. If we work *towards it*, we will inevitably strive to make it a reality here on earth. It will be seen as something distant and finally achievable only beyond this life. We may see glimmers of it today but only as a poor 'reflection' (1 Corinthians 13:12).

Alternatively, if we work *from it*, we will see it as a reality now. We will look instead to uncover and recognise that reality. We will look for its evidence now. We will look to see God's kingdom in heaven established on earth – now.

6 Presence and the enemy

The presence of God in our workplaces will not always be welcome. Some in the workplace will supernaturally discern the presence of the Holy Spirit within us, but that discernment does not always come from God.

6.1 His presence can bring a reaction

Jesus was recognised in this way:

> *In the synagogue there was a man possessed by a demon, an impure spirit. He cried out at the top of his voice, 'Go away! What do you want with us, Jesus of Nazareth? Have you come to destroy us? I know who you are – the Holy One of God!'* (Luke 4:33-34)

In 2008, my wife and I visited Finland with our pastor to assist with prayer ministry at a Christian conference. We stayed at a hotel during the week and I will not forget the reaction of one of the regular guests there, a lady in her forties. From the moment we arrived I sensed that she was agitated at our presence and over the week that agitation grew. Then, towards the end of the week, she cried out at the top of her voice, 'Oh no – not you again!'

Let us not be surprised or dismiss such reactions. It is too easy to explain a spiritual reaction in our places of work as a natural phenomenon. When we begin to recognise the presence of Father, Son and Holy Spirit in our places of work there is likely to be a reaction. In fact, the more confident we become of his presence, the more assured we become in our walk of faith and the more likely the enemy will respond in some way. Let us be on our guard. The apostle

Peter reminds us:

> *Be alert and of sober mind. Your enemy the devil prowls around like a roaring lion looking for someone to devour. Resist him, standing firm in the faith.* (1 Peter 5:8-9)

For a marketplace example, my wife, Margaret, visited the office where I worked. We have both liked to visit each other's workplaces occasionally. These visits would help in sharing our respective worlds. They would also communicate to other work colleagues that we were both in a committed lifelong relationship, offering our marriage a form of protection. Margaret's first encounter was with a senior executive whose reaction on meeting her was to exclaim, '*Oh, I hadn't realised Peter was married – you'd never have known.*' It was delivered as a joke – but we both felt that the remark also had about it the hallmark of the enemy.

6.2 *The enemy seeks to distract us from the presence*

What are some of the barriers to recognising the presence of God in the workplace? We have already named a few but I want us to focus for a moment on distractions. In *Disruptive Witness: Speaking the Truth in a Distracted Age*, Alan Noble talks about how technology (and especially the Internet and smartphones) can cause people to be both continually stimulated and distracted. He also describes the difficulties this presents in communicating Christian truth to others.

Hurriedness and distraction make it more difficult to be aware of God's presence

When we are distracted, or maybe, to use a biblical word, dissipated[22] (i.e. drawn in different directions), it is more difficult to become aware of the presence of God. We are too busy responding to other voices.

Self-awareness is an important part of recognising and addressing such distractions. We do well not to let ourselves become distracted or preoccupied by the work of the enemy in the workplace but instead, focus our attention on what the Father is doing in our places of work. For example, I recall an instance where an external marketing consultant had been hired by our company. The consultant had a reputation for creativity, dynamism and 'getting things done'. On one occasion he flew into an out-of-control rage at a business decision with which he did not agree. The incident made the national newspapers, but it would have been a mistake as a Christian to be overly preoccupied with such antics. The enemy was at work in that place but so was God.

22. See Luke 21:34.

7 Prayer

Let us conclude by considering again our response to the presence of God in the workplace using the prayer below.

Lord, forgive me when I doubt your presence in my place of work. Forgive me when I forget you, shut you out and operate in my place of work as though you do not exist. Forgive and have mercy on me.

Father, help me to know your presence with me. When surrounded by challenges that seem insurmountable, may I remember who you are and that my help comes from you, the Maker of heaven and earth. May I remember that all heaven and earth belong to you and that my place of work belongs to you also. Help me to carry that truth within.

Father, thank you for your presence in my work.

Jesus, help me to know your presence with me. Brother and friend – may I remember that you are able to sympathise with my weaknesses. You pick me up when I fall. You invite me to confide in you. You invite me to trust you. You bring challenge and encourage me to step out towards you. Teach me, as you taught your disciples, how to live for you in my place of work and to point others to you.

Lord Jesus, thank you for your presence in my work.

Holy Spirit, help me to know your presence within me. Form within me your fruitfulness today; that love, joy, peace, patience, kindness, goodness, faithfulness, gentleness and self-control. Guide me in my decisions and in my interactions with others. May I be attentive to your prompting, discerning your voice above the clamour of the noisy streets. Equip me with gifts and prompt me to use those gifts boldly; fanning them into flame for your purpose in my place of work. Give me courage to eagerly desire your gifts. May I see what you are already doing in my place of work and learn to cooperate with you to achieve your purpose.

Father, Son and Holy Spirit, thank you for your presence in my place of work.

Amen.

Chapter Three

Partnering with God in the Workplace

I pray that your partnership with us in the faith may be effective in deepening your understanding of every good thing we share for the sake of Christ.
(Philemon 1:6)

1 Introduction

We have looked at our purpose and God's presence so let us consider finally what it means to partner with God and others in our places of work.

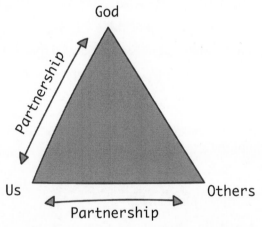

We exercise partnership both with God and others

As we shall see, God in his grace invites our partnership. We are also called to partner with others in our places of work, to cooperate or collaborate. Paul identifies this type of partnership in his letter to Philemon, cited above.

But let us pause for a moment and consider what an enormous privilege it is to partner with God in his work. We have looked at the presence of God in the workplace and there may be a sense in which we believe we are carrying the presence into our places of work. The truth is, however, that God is *already* active in our work environment – and invites us to partner with him in what he is *already* doing.

In 2017 I spent ten days in hospital for an operation to remove my appendix and a number of people in my local church were praying for me and my family. I had a profound sense of the presence of God in that place; it felt tangible. Over the ten days I saw inpatients come and go but there was one man, Tom, who caught my eye on the day I left. He sat alone on his chair and said these words: *'There's something really deep going on here and I can't make it out.'* To my knowledge this man was not a Christian but there was something in his spirit that caught a glimpse of what God was doing on that ward. We might call this a *'recognition of Eden'*. It is where a person recognises God at work. It is in this work that God invites our partnership.

2 Partnering with God

2.1 The God-initiated partnership

Let us consider the first work tasks given to Adam. The Lord took man and placed him in a delightful environment where he was to work the Garden and tend it.

The LORD God took the man and put him in the Garden of Eden to work it and take care of it. (Genesis 2:15)

From a very early age my father gave me and my three siblings jobs to do. We would get paid for the work and some of it was hard work: removing weeds, cutting the grass, assisting with house renovations. The process instilled within me an appreciation of work and reward. By the time I was sixteen I had worked – not always successfully – in several businesses; the most notable were a pet shop, fish and chip shop, fishing tackle shop and a mechanic's garage. My father helped find many of these jobs and did not criticise when, at times, I failed at the tasks given to me.

Our heavenly Father not only gives us work to do but invites our *partnership* with him in that same work.

> *Now the LORD God had formed out of the ground all the wild animals and all the birds in the sky. He brought them to the man to see what he would name them; and whatever the man called each living creature, that was its name.* (Genesis 2:19)

It's easy to miss the significance of this verse. There was a kind of a 'dance' in Eden; a partnership where humankind and God worked together. Let us note some features of this partnership.

Firstly, it was a *complementary* partnership. The Lord created and brought the living creatures to the Adam – and the Adam gave each a name. Adam would have been unable to do this without the Lord's interaction; the animals needed to be paraded before Adam so that the naming activity could take place. As we will see later in this section, this complementarity is still a feature of our partnership today, within the workplace.

Secondly, it was a *meaningful* partnership. The outcome of the creature-naming exercise was uncertain, for the Lord brought the animals to Adam to see the outcome. The partnership was genuine with both God and humankind playing a part. Or put another way, the man's contribution was meaningful and had significance. When the Lord invites us to partner with him in the workplace, both our contribution and the outcome will be meaningful and have significance.

Thirdly, it was *not a partnership of equals*. The Lord created all living creatures, including humankind, giving and sustaining all life. Adam was invited to partner with God, he bore God's image but he was not in any sense God's equal. Adam knew this as was evidenced when Satan tempted him with an apple from the tree of the knowledge of good and evil:

> *For God knows that when you eat from it your eyes will be opened, and you will be like God, knowing good and evil.* (Genesis 3:5)

This serves as a reminder to us that though we are invited to partner with God, it is not a partnership of equals. We may feel like this is stating the obvious, but in the context of discipleship within the Corinthian church, Paul makes the same observation:

> *I planted the seed, Apollos watered it, but God has been making it grow. So neither the one who plants nor the one who waters is anything, but only God, who makes things grow.* (1 Corinthians 3:6-7)

Fourthly, there are things that *sit outside* that partnership. The Lord invited the Adam to participate in partnership for a specific task. Adam was not invited to name the rivers, for instance, for that had already been done (Genesis 2:11-14). I do not think it a stretch to apply this to our own working lives. There are specific tasks which we are called to perform, there are others which we can influence (including by prayer) and there are some which are outside our domain. For example, it is the role of the Holy Spirit (and not us) to bring conviction of sin (John 16:8). Things do not go well when we try to do God's job for him!

And so, within this partnership that God offers, there is meaning to be found. This is God's design for yours, and my work today; God invites us to partner with Him in the work he gives us.

What does this look like in practice? I believe it involves a daily conversation with God *as we go about* our work. *'Lord, I've a tricky meeting planned today, how do you want me to prepare for it?' 'Jesus, I can see that my friend at work is troubled by something. Give me a listening ear and words of encouragement for him. Is there anything, Lord, you want to say to him?'* Whilst this question to the Lord may be of a pastoral nature, it can equally be strategic: *'Lord, what are you saying to us about the direction for our organisation?'*

These prayers, you may notice, are less 'arrow prayers asking for help' and are more a dialogue with the Holy Spirit, asking for guidance and practical wisdom. These prayers can be 'tactical', concerning immediate issues of the day, or they can be 'strategic' in the sense of addressing longer-term and broader matters in our workplaces.

2.2 Partnership is based on the covenant of love

Nehemiah had a plan to rebuild the walls of Jerusalem driven by his desire to restore the people's national pride. Now, we have to remember that nowhere in Scripture does God promise to help the people build the walls surrounding the city. So what was the basis of Nehemiah's appeal to God as he prays for God's help in the rebuilding project?

LORD, *the God of heaven, the great and awesome God, who keeps his covenant of love with those who love him and keep his commandments, let your ear be attentive and your eyes open to hear the prayer your servant is praying before you.* (Nehemiah 1:5-6)

The basis of his prayer was the '*covenant of love*'. He knew that God is committed to his people; God is concerned about what matters to them. This is partnership in action. God is interested in our work and partners with us about the things that matter to us as Christians.

> Let us be confident that our work matters to God, that it has purpose in itself, that we can partner with God as we go about our work and that we bring to our work meaning by virtue of his image within us. God invites us to partner with him on the basis of a covenant of love.

2.3 Partnership – *is it two-way?*

I want us to look at the pages of Scripture and ask whether, when we partner with God, is this a case of 'us partnering with his purpose' or 'him partnering with ours'? For some this might be a surprising question, so let us look further.

In Genesis, Scripture records that Abram had no sons. In the context of that culture, this would have brought shame on Sarai his wife. It also meant that a servant within his household would inherit his estate.

The word of the LORD came to Abram in a vision: 'Do not be afraid, Abram. I am your shield, your very great reward.' But Abram said, 'Sovereign LORD, what can you give me since I remain childless and the one who will inherit my estate is Eliezer of Damascus?' And Abram said, 'You have given me no children; so a servant in my household will be my heir.' Then the word of the LORD came to him: 'This man will not be your heir, but a son who is your own flesh and blood will be your heir.' He took him outside and said, 'Look up at the sky and count the stars – if indeed you can count them.' Then he said to him, 'So shall your offspring be.' Abram believed the LORD, and he credited it to him as righteousness. (Genesis 15:1-6)

Now the Lord could have ignored the conventions and culture of the day but because family lineage was important to Abram, it was important to the Lord. He promised Abram offspring as numerous as the stars in the sky. Again, we might have argued that the Lord himself would be Abram's source of significance – but instead the Lord gave Abram a promise that would mean he would have significance beyond his wildest imagination. Abram did not see the fullness of this come to fruition. It did not occur in his lifetime. But he believed the promise and goodness of God and this was credited to him as righteousness.

So how does this relate to our places of work? God knows our work culture and knows what matters to us, and because it matters to us, it matters to him. So it is an important question to ask ourselves: what matters to me in my place of work?

When we partner with God, we are engaging with him *in his work*. It could be that we are motivated and compelled to do this work and maybe that sense of compulsion comes from our faith and originates within the mind of God. In these cases, the *work we do is in alignment with God's purpose*. God is always the initiator.

But there is another feature at work here. God, in his love for us, is interested in us and in what is on our hearts. Does the Creator of the universe choose to align his purpose with ours? At times, if we reflect honestly about our work, this is what we want from God; we want him to align his purpose with ours. We want him to 'come on board' with our plans and to 'make them happen'.

Part of this desire, however, stems from a limited understanding of God's purpose in the first place. In other words, if we believe that God is primarily interested in 'church activities', then we are left with two alternatives: either we believe God is not interested in our workplaces at all or we ask him to intervene in our workplaces and 'align his purpose with ours'.

The reality, however, is that he is already active in our places of work and intimately interested in our working lives, in all its aspects. So, whilst we might be tempted to 'persuade God' to act on our behalf in fulfilling *our* purpose, what is really needed is an expanded vision of *his* purpose for our places of work. We are called to come on board with his plans, not him with ours. In this instance, too, we see God is always the initiator.

Let's observe this in Scripture. 2 Thessalonians 1:11 says:

> *We constantly pray for you, that our God may make you worthy of his calling, and that by his power he may bring to fruition your every desire for goodness and your every deed prompted by faith.*

Paul prayed that God would bring fruit from the work they were doing. However, we read also that their work *flowed from their faith* and so we can be assured that there was an alignment between God's purpose and that of the Thessalonians. It was God's purpose that was being fulfilled, not humankind's.

Similarly, for us, if our workplace actions are prompted by faith and goodness, then we can be more confident that our purpose is aligned with God's; that God will partner with us and bring fruit from our work.

2.4 As we partner we learn to trust despite the darkness

Partnering with God is not always about navigating a path strewn with clearly labelled signposts. God may call us to walk along unfamiliar paths. It is there that he offers a promise:

I will lead the blind by ways they have not known, along unfamiliar paths I will guide them; I will turn the darkness into light before them and make the rough places smooth. These are the things I will do; I will not forsake them. (Isaiah 42:16)

When I was made redundant after years working in one company, the future seemed very uncertain. Our family finances were challenged and the future appeared far from clear. I felt like I was feeling my way in the darkness, unsure of what lay ahead and fearful of the future. The Lord led me to read books on the subject of trust and one thing that he taught me has remained ever since: *the darkness is not always a bad place to be.*

My goal at that time was to remove the darkness of uncertainty and step out into the well-signposted light. Life just isn't like that. God was teaching me that when I was in the darkness I could learn to trust him more. Trust develops faith.

In our partnership with God in the workplace there will be plenty of uncertain times. We need to treasure these times and not see them as blights on the landscape or roadblocks on the path. They are God-given opportunities to develop greater levels of trust.

2.5 In partnership we find out what pleases God

Ephesians 5:10 exhorts us to '*find out what pleases the Lord*'. God does not hide from us his pleasure and it can be found in the workplace. Paul's writing suggests that we each have a responsibility to understand what pleases the Lord. Much of our partnership with God concerns understanding the will of God and following it, or put another way, '*find[ing] out what pleases the Lord*' (Ephesians 5:10).

Ruth, a senior management trainer, was pitching for a new piece of work with a client. She spent some time beforehand listening to God in prayer and asking him how she should approach the pitch. Ruth had a clear sense that she needed to let the client set the level for her fees. This was an unusual, 'risky' approach in her industry and certainly counter-cultural. Ruth wrestled in prayer over the guidance she had received but eventually decided to act on God's leading.

When we listen to the Holy Spirit, he will sometimes lead us places we would not normally go

When it came to the pitch, the client asked Ruth what her fees were, to which Ruth responded, '*I'd like you to pay what you can afford.*' The client was impressed. '*You don't know how refreshing it is to hear that*,' came the reply. The interviewer continued, '*We had another client drive for very high rates which we eventually agreed to, but they are not going to get any work from us.*' Ruth was offered the work.[23]

When we listen to God, walking in partnership with him, he may lead us in counter-cultural ways. When we obey in response to his leading, fruitfulness will follow and God's pleasure is the result.

---

23. This story is told in more detail in Greene, Mark, *The One About... 8 Stories About God in Our Everyday* (LICC, 2018).

2.6 With partnership comes provision

Earlier, I mentioned about my time in hospital for an operation. During the ten days I was there God spoke to me like at no other time. He gave specific guidance about questions I was already asking. Should I move house? When should we move? The Lord said that March would be a significant month. January came and went and I remembered the word given to me. *'Lord, is that March this year, or another year?'* was my prayer. Silence followed. At the end of February our marketing director, my immediate boss, resigned. On 1st March, I was called into a meeting with the executive director of my company. The question put to me was, *'How do you see your future here and what opportunities would you like to explore?'* This was too much of a coincidence to ignore and so I pushed a door that had remained closed up to that time. *'I would like to work remotely, from home.'* My wife and I had been praying about a move to Sheffield for some time but the logistics of moving home, church, community and job all at the same time seemed insurmountable. Working remotely would have given me an opportunity to move house whilst having an important element in my life stable: my job. The executive director said yes, and we moved house later that year.

God provides for us as our loving heavenly Father when we partner with him. This, of course, is not an occasional event in our Christian lives. God invites us to trust him for his provision daily.

In our places of work, opportunities abound to trust him for his provision: to trust him for our finances, our reward and our recognition, to trust him for guidance and to trust him for wisdom in making decisions.

At work, we have the opportunity to trust God for our reward and recognition

2.7 Partnership obscured

Back to Genesis, and after the Fall we see a difference in the way humankind related to God. Firstly, Adam was afraid of God and ashamed of his sin.

I heard you in the garden, and I was afraid because I was naked; so I hid. (Genesis 3:10)

When Adam and Eve were eventually banished from the garden we can see how their children Cain and Abel sought God's favour by offering a sacrifice. The partnership that we saw with Adam was still in evidence, but it was now *obscured* from Adam; he and his offspring had only an uncertain assurance of God's favour and any partnership had anxieties because of that uncertainty.

What impact does this have today in our workplaces? In our *natural state*, we have little assurance of the favour of God as we go about our work and certainly little appreciation of partnership with him. However, as Christians this has changed. We are given, through God's grace, his unmerited favour and *the work we do now stems from the certain position of this favour.*

> The invitation to partner with God remains unchanged, but it is now no longer obscured by uncertainty.

When we were children, our natural inclination was to seek the favour of our earthly parents. We sought their love and affirmation. When we became Christians, we naturally transposed this same approach to our heavenly Father. We sought the Father's favour, often by acts of service. However, in practice, partnership has a very different feel. In partnership we enjoy our work *'with God'* as opposed to *'for God'* and we work knowing his favour, rather than working for his favour. I believe this position of partnership is what Jesus meant when he said to his disciples,

> *You are my friends if you do what I command. I no longer call you servants, because a servant does not know his master's business. Instead, I have called you friends, for everything that I learned from my Father I have made known to you.* (John 15:14-15)

Jesus called his disciples 'friends' (and therefore, by implication, partners with him in his work).

2.8 Partnership in rest

There is one aspect of partnership that we have not yet covered and that is the matter of rest. After God created the earth, on the seventh day he rested. God rested and he later commanded the people to rest.

> *Remember the Sabbath day by keeping it holy. Six days you shall labour and do all your work, but the seventh*

day is a sabbath to the LORD your God. On it you shall not do any work . . . For in six days the LORD made the heavens and the earth, the sea, and all that is in them, but he rested on the seventh day. Therefore the LORD blessed the Sabbath day and made it holy. (Exodus 20:8-11)

Since this is a book about work, I did not begin with a discussion about rest. However, if we look closely at the Genesis account, we can see that this is not how God designed the order of things. God finished the work of Creation in six days and on the seventh he rested. Adam was made on day six and so Adam's *first* experience of life within Creation was that of rest. Historically, rest came first and work followed afterwards.

Rest, I believe, is designed to be restorative and regenerative and is part of God's plan for our lives as Christians. If we want to partner with God in our places of work then we need both to understand the importance of and to prioritise rest. Rest was Adam's first day and work followed; so too for us. Rest is designed to be a reservoir from which we can draw strength during our working week.

Whilst Sabbath rests are God's blueprint for all of Creation, we can see from the text below that God works all the time.

Because Jesus was doing these things on the Sabbath, the Jewish leaders began to persecute him. In his defence Jesus said to them, 'My Father is always at his work to this very day, and I too am working.' (John 5:16-17)

We can rest on the Sabbath in the knowledge that God works for us in sustaining the universe; that is not our job!

John Mark Comer, in his book *Garden City*, adds a number of practices to Sabbath observation; those of silence, solitude, simplicity and slowing (down). The Sabbath provides an opportunity for us to connect more deeply with God; a vital element of partnering with him in work on the remaining six days.

Finally, when we take rest we not only give space to reconnect with God in a deeper way but we model rest to others. Let me share an example.

I was on the leadership team in a small organisation in the south of England. The head of human resources noted that many of the employees in the organisation seemed worn out and stressed. Work was demanding, hours were long and expectations high. We agreed as a team to purchase a pool table which would sit in the foyer of our building. The idea was to give natural opportunities for recreation within the work environment. The pool table arrived and for a number of weeks sat unused. The CEO asked why this was and I replied that no-one had seen one of the executive directors using it. I sensed that people were reticent about being seen to take 'time out' because it had not been legitimised or modelled by those in authority. Within two weeks that changed and positive results were seen.

Others will observe and take note how we model rest and recreation in our lives

The point I want to make is that whether it be recreation (in this example) or rest, the choices we make as individuals and followers of Jesus will serve *as a model to colleagues* in our workplace. Others will take note and follow as we observe the biblical mandate to take rest.

2.9 The benefits of partnership

As we have seen, when we partner with God we are called to take rest. Let us now turn to the benefits of our partnership with God.

> The book of Ecclesiastes puts it like this: 'Two are better than one, because they have a good return for their labour.' (Ecclesiastes 4:9)

There are two benefits of partnership that I want to explore further: partnering when we face *opposition* and partnering when we feel *overwhelmed*.

Nehemiah faced a formidable task of rebuilding the city walls of Jerusalem. He requested the release of resources from those in authority so that he could complete the task (Nehemiah 2:8) and also identified a team of individuals who would partner with him (Nehemiah 2:17-18). Shortly after the start of the project there came opposition in the form of ridicule and scheming (Nehemiah 4:1 and 4:8).

God invites us to partner with him in his work. This invitation is particularly important when it comes to opposition that we will inevitably face.

> The Lord will partner with us whenever we face opposition in the workplace when we invite him to do so.

Whenever we face opposition in the workplace, we can choose to partner ourselves with God. The opposition might remain, but our perspective will change

For a New Testament example of opposition, consider Paul's letter to Timothy. Paul experienced considerable opposition from Alexander and whilst he received no support from others, he received strength directly from God:

Alexander the metalworker did me a great deal of harm . . . You too should be on your guard against him, because he strongly opposed our message. At my first defence, no one came to my support, but everyone deserted me. May it not be held against them. But the Lord stood at my side and gave me strength. (2 Timothy 4:14-17)

Paul was partnering with God in his work and received help when he faced opposition. We can have the same hope and expectation in our places of work.

Let us now turn to the question of fatigue. Nehemiah also faced fatigue in his workplace project and he turns this into an opportunity to pray.

They were all trying to frighten us, thinking, 'Their hands will get too weak for the work, and it will not be completed.' But I prayed, 'Now strengthen my hands.' (Nehemiah 6:9)

At times of exhaustion, we can ask for God's strength and help

There will be times when we are weary and fatigued in our places of work. In these circumstances we might, like Nehemiah, offer a prayer asking for strength. Or we might ask God to walk with us each step of the journey in what becomes a desire for his fellowship. In these circumstances the elements of the task might not change, but there is a sweetness of knowing that he walks with us in the challenges we face.

2.10 Summary

In summary, we have considered the following:

❖ God invites us to partner with him in our places of work. He is already there and his desire is that we align our purpose with his.

❖ God's commitment to us is based on a 'covenant of love'. In the workplace, he blesses 'every act prompted by faith'.

❖ God graciously works with our (sanctified) purposes in the workplace.

❖ We can learn to trust God not just when the direction is clear, but in the absence of a clear understanding of the way forward.

❖ As we partner with God, we learn what brings him delight and pleases him. As a loving heavenly Father, we can trust him to meet our needs, including in our places of work.

❖ Sabbath rests are an indispensable element of partnering with God and present an opportunity to connect more deeply with God.

❖ Partnership with God is particularly helpful whenever we face opposition in the workplace or when we feel overwhelmed by the enormity of the task ahead of us.

3 Partnering with others

God invites us to partner with him. This is a privilege and joy. We are also called to partner with others; to work in cooperation with our co-workers. This of course brings many challenges and opportunities to learn. I would like to mention just a few of those learning opportunities as it pertains to the workplace. It is worth mentioning that partnership with colleagues brings challenges for us all. Many people are fearful to partner with others, concerned that their vulnerabilities and weaknesses will be exposed and even exploited. Patrick Lencioni has written books[24] that explore in the

---

24. For example, Lencioni, Patrick, *The Five Dis-functions of a Team* (John Wiley & Sons, 2002) and Lencioni, Patrick, *Silos, Politics and Turf Wars* (Jossey-Bass, 2006).

form of fables, the problems that arise when people do not partner well with one another.

Unless we partner well with others, dysfunction is the result

3.1 As we partner with others, we both 'go high' and 'go low'

As we partner with others we both 'go high' and 'go low'. 'Go high' concerns our assurance of our standing before God and its fruit is faith and confidence. 'Go low' concerns our calling to serve others and its fruit is humility and sacrifice.

'Go high' is the perspective that we are in Christ as we go about our work. All authority in heaven and on earth was given to Jesus and that same spiritual authority has now been given to us. We have authority over Creation. We have authority in the spiritual realm. We have the authority of God's truth. We have been given the promises of God and we have the discernment of God's Spirit within us.

'Go low' is the perspective that we are servants as we go about our work. We are called to serve others just as Jesus did. We have a sense of duty as we go about our work, not looking for reward or thanks. The world might talk of 'rights' and 'entitlements' but as followers of Jesus we know these need to be reconsidered.

For the following two stories, I have named the individuals Sam and Pat. These names are purposely gender-neutral to avoid stereotypes. The point being that 'go low' is neither a male nor female mandate; nor is 'go high'.

Sam was operating in 'go high' mode and approached the place of work with confidence knowing that God had given a calling to be salt and light in the work environment. Sam prayed on entering the building for God's blessing on work colleagues, confident in the knowledge of the presence of Jesus through the Holy Spirit. Sam's job security was in God's hands and little thought was given to financial 'worries'. God had provided in the past and had promised to provide for Sam and the family in the future. Sam prayed quietly, *'Lord, guide me today, by your Holy Spirit. May I shine for you. May I speak your words today. Give me wisdom in the decisions I make.'*

Not everything went smoothly but Sam was less rattled by the unexpected than in the past. The first response to the unexpected was to turn thoughts upward. *'Lord, what are you saying to me in this?'* and *'How do you want me to respond to this, Lord?'*

When Sam faced opposition in work including internal politics, Sam was less confrontational than others in the department. Again, Sam prayed about difficult characters in the workplace. *'Lord, what are you teaching me here?'* and *'What do you want to draw my attention to through this encounter, Lord?'*

Sam walked, clothed in the armour of God. Sam demolished spiritual strongholds and claimed territory to advance the kingdom in the workplace.

It was Monday morning and Pat was operating in 'go low' mode. Pat was a faithful worker who worked tirelessly in the business, putting the interests of the company before personal ambitions. Pat was quick to acknowledge the contribution of others in the team. When praise came for work completed, this was always a pleasant surprise for Pat but Pat was never deflected by it. Pat wanted to serve God in the place of work and had entrusted God with matters of honour and reputation.

Two modes of operating – we are called to both

When facing opposition, Pat exhibited a calmness and peace. Many attributed this to disposition but in reality it was because Pat had learned over time to deal with personal pride. Pat *acted justly, loved mercy and walked humbly with God* (see Micah 6:8). Pat's faith was expressed both internally and externally – seeking to serve others and do what was right in the organisation, whilst listening to the Holy Spirit for guidance and direction.

Here we have two models of operating. My point is that we are called to walk in both modes as we exercise the servant leadership demonstrated by Jesus.

The emphasis of 'Go High' is confident assurance in our standing before God. We are bold and confident in our prayers. We are ambitious for God's Kingdom. We are determined. A key verse for us is,

In Christ you have been brought to fullness. (Colossians 2:10)

In 'Go Low' mode we recognise our frailties. We are self-aware and know our weaknesses. Our emphasis is on service to others. A key verse for us is,

The Son of Man did not come to be served, but to serve. (Mark 10:45)

Of course, both are true and other verses of Scripture can be found in their support. We are both sons and daughters of the living God and also servants of all. When we partner with God in our places of work, we are called to demonstrate both of these perspectives.

3.2 When we partner with others, we can call out God's image

We each bear the image of God within us, whether or not we are a follower of Jesus. If we ask God to reveal his image, we can see that image in all humankind and our workplaces bring an opportunity to both see this image and 'call it out'.

The challenge for many of us is not so much to see the image but to know what to do when it is revealed. Let us look at how Jesus recognises the God-image in the woman at the well. Jesus said to her:

> *You are right when you say you have no husband. The fact is, you have had five husbands, and the man you now have is not your husband. What you have just said is quite true.* (John 4:17-18)

Jesus commends her for her honesty whilst choosing to not pass judgement on her lifestyle. Many of our colleagues are looking for someone who recognises the God-image in them, whilst not condemning them for their shortcomings. Such encounters can be significant and rewarding when conducted in the workplace.

I often use the phrase, '*I really like the way you . . .*' and then to recognise or 'call out' some God-attribute within the person. It's transformational and not difficult to do.

In Luke 7:9 we read of an encounter Jesus had with a centurion.

> *Jesus . . . was amazed at him, and turning to the crowd following him, he said, 'I tell you, I have not found such great faith even in Israel.'*

Jesus called out the centurion's faith and we can do the same at work. It may not be faith we call out, it may be some other godly attribute.

When we call out positive attributes in others, we not only recognise the image of God in the person but draw others' attention to it. This brings great encouragement to our work colleagues as well as serving to remind us that we each bear God's image.

3.3 As we partner with others we work on their agenda

There is danger if we have a partnering-with-God mind-set whilst forgetting that at the same time we are called to work with others. There are even times when others' agenda might not align with our personal values and yet still we are called to serve.

When we partner with others, we may need to work with them on their plan

Daniel was a man of God who lived in a foreign land subject to laws and customs which did not align with his own. Daniel addressed the matter of his diet. His approach was not belligerent. Instead, we know:

Daniel resolved not to defile himself with the royal food and wine, and he asked the chief official for permission not to defile himself in this way. (Daniel 1:8)

In other words, Daniel was subject to the laws of his day and acted respectfully to those in authority over him. He proposed a plan to eat only vegetables, and pleaded with the official, *'Please test [us] for ten days'* (Daniel 1:12).

When the plan worked and the appearance of Daniel and his colleagues was better than that of those who had eaten the royal food, the young men were taken away and placed on a programme of learning. During this time they will have learned much about the culture and customs of this foreign country.

Many of us will feel as though we are foreigners and strangers in a working world. The organisation we work for may advocate customs and practices that do not sit comfortably with our Christian values. Sometimes we might be called out of a workplace where its values are extreme but, for the most part, many of us are called to stay. God knows our hearts. If we respond with humility, God will bless.

Daniel had such a response. When he and his companions were sent on an education programme we find:

To these four young men God gave knowledge and understanding of all kinds of literature and learning. And Daniel could understand visions and dreams of all kinds. (Daniel 1:17)

This was 'education-plus': God added to their education programme. When we work with humility and are prepared to work with others on their agenda, God takes notice.

Sherman and Hendricks make the point that the goal of partnering with others will be undermined if we use it to serve religious aims: i.e. if we perceive our work *'simply as a platform for proclaiming the gospel, then we will come to work, not to work, but to proclaim the gospel'.*[25]

---

25. Some content taken from Sherman, Doug and Hendricks, William, *Your Work Matters to God*, p. 71. Copyright © 1987. Used by permission of NavPress, represented by Tyndale House Publishers, a Division of Tyndale House Ministries. All rights reserved.

They go on to say that there is a danger: our participation in work becomes both half-hearted and misaligned with workplace objectives. The alternative, of course, is to work with others *on their agenda*.

The final point of note is that for Daniel and his friends, at the end of their programme they entered the king's service. We might look upon this and emphasise the word 'king', that is to say, it was a privileged position – and it was. But equally, we could emphasise the word 'service' and note that despite all their learning and God's anointing, they were called to be servants.

Some of us may feel over qualified for the tasks given to us. The manner in which we respond to these challenges is significant for the tasks might be preparatory. God often has something bigger in mind, as he had with Daniel.

3.4 As we partner with others, we bear up under the pain of unjust suffering

When we partner with others in our place of work, there will be injustices. For instance, people and their contributions will get overlooked. In fact, in the workplaces, injustices abound.

Now sometimes God may be prompting us to speak out in response to an injustice. At other times, we are called to bear up under injustices. In the latter instance, we can note:

> *It is commendable if someone bears up under the pain of unjust suffering because they are conscious of God.* (1 Peter 2:19)

In our places of work, we are usually on safe ground as Christians if we speak up *on behalf of others* for the injustice they face. If we are facing a personal injustice, we need to ask ourselves before God, 'Am I to speak up or bear up?'

There have been times when I have gone for the latter rather than the former and I can think of situations that in hindsight I would have chosen differently, choosing to speak up respectfully, but assertively.

3.5 As we partner we learn to forgive

The subject of forgiveness is vast and I will not attempt to cover it in detail here. Other books, *Total Forgiveness*[26] and *Grace and Forgiveness*,[27] tackle the subject in some depth. I would like, however, to consider the subject as it pertains to the workplace and will make a few observations.

Firstly, we may have been wronged at work but it is worth remembering that organisations themselves cannot be judged to have sinned. Only individuals sin and can be judged by God of wrongdoing. It is true that a group of individuals may collectively act in sinful ways, but I do not believe there is a separate moral entity before God called an 'organisation'.

Now there are instances in Scripture when a group of people is collectively judged by God, but I believe this is because of the *weight* of wrongdoing within that group. Jesus said, for instance:

> Woe to you, Chorazin! Woe to you, Bethsaida! For if the miracles that were performed in you had been performed in Tyre and Sidon, they would have repented long ago, sitting in sackcloth and ashes. (Luke 10:13)

These two towns were condemned by Jesus for their unbelief. But there were still *individuals* from these towns that were exempt from

---

26. Kendal, R.T., *Total Forgiveness* (Hodder & Stoughton, 2003).
27. Arnott, John and Carol, *Grace and Forgiveness* (New Wine Press, 2009).

this judgement by Jesus; Peter, Philip and Andrew, for instance, were all from Bethsaida.

In practice for us, we may feel justified in pronouncing a judgement on an organisation for the way they have treated us. But quite apart from the fact that we are called not to judge others, I want to point out that it is individuals and not organisations who require our forgiveness.

When we feel aggrieved by our employer, we may be tempted to exercise anger, unforgiveness and vengeance

When we exercise forgiveness, it needs always to be directed *to a person or persons*. People may have grieved us and caused hurt and pain. The longer our working lives, the more opportunity we will have to exercise God's grace of forgiveness.

In practice, when we partner with others in our places of work, we will inevitably experience some injustices causing us personal hurt and pain. In the process of forgiveness it is useful to recognise the specific people involved and to prayerfully forgive them, by name. This process might involve our choosing not to stand in judgement over others.

When I was made redundant on one occasion I felt angry. I was determined, however, not to become bitter and it took two years before the feelings of resentment totally subsided. I had to actively name and forgive the individuals concerned, praying blessing over their lives (whether or not I felt this was deserved). This had the effect of both releasing them and freeing me from the negative effects of bitterness. As Hebrews instructs us:

See to it that no one falls short of the grace of God and that no bitter root grows up to cause trouble and defile many. (Hebrews 12:15)

Secondly, much forgiveness exercised by Christians in the workplace will necessarily be *unilateral*. By this I mean that those in authority may sin against us and cause us harm. But apologies may never arrive, and wrongs may never be acknowledged. It remains our responsibility, however, to initiate forgiveness for others in our places of work. In practice this could involve a threefold approach: asking God to help us forgive, looking to recognise good qualities in those who have hurt us and praying blessing (however much we feel it is undeserved) over their lives. Jesus said:

I tell you, love your enemies and pray for those who persecute you, that you may be children of your Father in heaven. (Matthew 5:44-45)

3.6 We partner undefended and transparent

When we partner with others we partner in a battlefield and not a playground. Shortly after the launch of the book *Fruitfulness on the Frontline*[28] I heard some suggest that the title is too militaristic. I think not. We are entering a battlefield in our places of work. The enemy will attack us and at times we will get hurt by others with whom we partner.

I want us to consider the notion of being both undefended and transparent. Let us take these in turn.

By undefended, I mean that when we partner with others we do not expend efforts in guarding our own reputation. As we follow Christ, we may be misunderstood or even maligned within our organisation. Jesus himself gave us an example to follow.

> *When they hurled their insults at him, he did not retaliate; when he suffered, he made no threats. Instead, he entrusted himself to him who judges justly.* (1 Peter 2:23)

And elsewhere, in the Psalms:

> *My salvation and my honour depend on God; he is my mighty rock, my refuge.* (Psalm 62:7)

> *Trust in him at all times, you people; pour out your hearts to him, for God is our refuge.* (Psalm 62:8)

There may be instances where we believe the Holy Spirit is prompting us to speak up in our own defence; to clarify matters so that misunderstandings do not arise. In these instances, the promise

---

28. Greene, Mark, *Fruitfulness on the Frontline: Making a Difference Where You Are* (IVP, 2014).

of Scripture that God will *'refute every tongue that accuses you'* (Isaiah 54:17) might involve us having a part to play.

For the most part, however, I believe that as Christians we are called to live *undefended*. In this we will inevitably stand out from our colleagues. The fruit of this approach is that we will not waste time on self-justification or apportioning blame and at the same time we will grow in our trust of God, that he will vindicate our position.

Secondly, let us consider transparency. We may be urged by Christian friends to live transparent lives before others; to be unapologetic about our faith, our values and how we spend our time. Certainly Jesus talked about our clearly identifying with him, including in our places of work.

If anyone is ashamed of me and my words in this adulterous and sinful generation, the Son of Man will be ashamed of them when he comes in his Father's glory with the holy angels. (Mark 8:38)

The standard is clear. We need to be bold and unafraid – and if we feel fearful, we can ask for the help of the Holy Spirit to overcome that fear.

For the Spirit God gave us does not make us timid, but gives us power, love and self-discipline. (2 Timothy 1:7)

There is, however, a further consideration. When we live lives in partnership with others at work, we also need to be wise in what we share of our lives – listening to the Holy Spirit as to what and to whom we share the Truth. This wisdom needs not to be motivated by fear of disclosure but out of concern of the consequences. In the Sermon on the Mount, Jesus described the dangers of entrusting precious teaching (the pearls) to those who would be disdainful of its true value (the dogs and pigs).

Do not give dogs what is sacred; do not throw your pearls to pigs.
If you do, they may trample them under their feet, and turn and
tear you to pieces. (Matthew 7:6)

For many of us in Western cultures, this is not a situation we face. But we do need to be mindful that self-disclosure in some nations carries with it a risk of personal safety. Context for self-disclosure, of course, is important too.

3.7 Not all partners will share our values

When we partner with others we will be aware that not all partners share our values. I want to focus, however, on where conflicts arise because of personal ambition in the workplace.

Some of our colleagues (and indeed ourselves) will be motivated by a desire for influence. This, I believe, is a relatively benign motivator. People want their contribution in the workplace to make impact and to 'count'. The advantage of this motivation is that it allows others to respond to such contribution and choose to be influenced.

Other colleagues will be motivated by a desire for control. This, I believe, can be more destructive to those in their path. In this situation, people want to enhance their own position in an organisation at the *expense of others* and sometimes at the *expense of the organisation* itself. This falls under the category of 'selfish ambition'. James warns us:

Who is wise and understanding among you? Let them show it
by their good life, by deeds done in the humility that comes from
wisdom. But if you harbour bitter envy and selfish ambition
in your hearts, do not boast about it or deny the truth. Such

'wisdom' does not come down from heaven but is earthly, unspiritual, demonic. (James 3:13-15)

It is interesting to note the source of such behaviour and James identifies this in the strongest possible terms; it is demonic. This gives us an indication as to how to respond to such behaviour.

We can often dismiss it as a matter of temperament or personality but James suggests that its source is spiritual. Our response therefore needs to involve the use of the tools available to us as Christians:

For though we live in the world, we do not wage war as the world does. The weapons we fight with are not the weapons of the world. On the contrary, they have divine power to demolish strongholds. (2 Corinthians 10:3-4)

Prayer is available to us when we meet such challenges.

The other part of the verse in James talks about 'envy' and for many of us as Christians, this temptation is a lot closer to home. R.T. Kendal suggests that both jealousy and envy are much more prevalent than we might think.[29] Solomon wrote:

I saw that all toil and all achievement spring from one person's envy of another. (Ecclesiastes 4:4)

For this we need to check our own hearts so that we are not ensnared by the subtlety of envy.

Prayer, then, offers us hope. It provides a means by which we can know the heart of God in response to the ambitions of others in our places of work. It also is the means for examining our own motivations so as to ensure we are not driven by envy of others.

---

29. Kendal, R.T., *Jealousy: The Sin No-one Talks About* (Hodder & Stoughton, 2011).

3.8 We partner as broken people with other broken people

Lastly, we need to remember that when we partner with others we partner as 'broken' people with other 'broken' people.

I had been working in a new role for eighteen months when I noticed that one of my senior colleagues verbally undermined others in our meetings.

In this case I asked God to intervene to end the put-downs and that I might develop a deeper understanding and appreciation of my colleague.

> *Whoever derides their neighbour has no sense, but the one who has understanding holds their tongue.* (Proverbs 11:12)

The effects of this approach might be seen as short term – focusing on behaviour in a given meeting – but it does recognise that at times there may be a spiritual issue underlying someone's behaviour in the workplace.

3.9 Summary

Our final summary is as follows:

❖ When we work with others and partner with them, we will do well to have attitudes of 'go high' and 'go low'.

❖ The workplace gives opportunity to recognise the God-image in others and call it out.

❖ It is important that when we partner with others we work with them on their agenda and avoid the bear traps of deceit and manipulation.

❖ Workplace situations give great opportunities to learn to bear up under unjust suffering and to learn to forgive, even if a wrongdoing has not been acknowledged.

❖ Let us be aware of the ambitions of others in the workplace. Where these ambitions are questionable, this calls for wisdom from God as to how best to respond.

❖ We partner as broken people and with broken people. This calls for humility and discernment in working with others.

4 Prayer

The following prayer concerns partnership both with God and others. I believe we cannot isolate the two.

Lord, thank you that you invite us to partner with you in what you are doing in our world and in my place of work. Give me spiritual insight to see what you are doing and the roles you are calling me to fulfil. Lord, I pray for your equipping to do your work; for skill and wisdom.

Lord, there are times, too, when you lay something on my heart with regards to the workplace. Help me discern this inner voice and to know how to respond to it.

Lord, you call us also to partner with others. Lord, make me like a Daniel, who was found neither to be corrupt nor negligent. Work, Lord, in my relationships and interactions with others. I pray your blessings now on my work colleagues.

In Jesus' name I pray. Amen.

Chapter Four

Conclusion

Now all has been heard; here is the conclusion of the matter: fear God
and keep his commandments, for this is the duty of all mankind.
(Ecclesiastes 12:13)

We have considered faith in the workplace from three angles: the purpose of God, the presence of God and partnering with God.

There is a great deal of literature written from a Christian perspective that addresses the subject of purpose. When it comes to presence, an oft-quoted source is Brother Lawrence's book where he describes the practice of seeking God's presence whilst sweeping leaves off the kitchen floor.[30]

For partnership, there is a notable gap in Christian literature as it relates to the workplace. The same could be said of a perspective that recognises the workplace as a battlefield in which the enemy is active. For instance, Derek Prince, in his writings talks a great deal about spiritual conflict but not as it relates to the workplace.

When this is the case, we would be wise to check what we are reading against the balance of Scripture. I believe I have sought to reflect such a balance in this short book but would urge you to weigh the arguments with this in mind.

---

30. Brother Lawrence, *The Practice of the Presence of God* (Leyland Edwards, 2018).

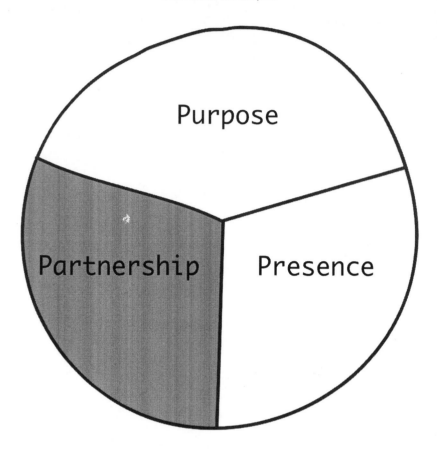

Partnership provides an opportunity to work with an expanded vision for our work

The notions of purpose, presence and partnership are inter-dependent. We are all motivated by a desire for purpose and this can be found by both recognising the presence of God in our places of work and by working in partnership with him.

Our inheritance as Christians lies in Eden. Here, Adam and Eve understood God's purpose, they experienced God's presence, and partnered with him in bearing his image and extending his kingdom. As believers, this remains God's invitation to us today.

Prayer

This is a prayer of declaration and blessing over you.

In the name of Jesus, I declare that you are God's workmanship, created in Christ Jesus to do good works, which God prepared in advance for you to do.

As a servant of the King, you are inheritors of every spiritual blessing in Christ.

May you be strenghthened with power through God's Spirit in your inner being so that Christ may dwell in your hearts through faith.

May God equip you with every good thing for doing his will.

Whatever you do, whether in word or deed, do it in the name of Jesus, working at it with all your heart, as working for the Lord and not for human masters.

May God bless you and make you a blessing in your place of work.

Amen.

Questions for Group Discussion

Purpose

1. Adam and Eve were called by God to be image-bearers. How does this perspective affect the way you see your work?

2. Do you have a sense of purpose in your work? If so – what is it?

3. To what extent do you seek out identity in the work you do? What are the potential downsides to this?

4. What practical steps can we take to work from our identity and not towards it?

5. What do you believe is God's vision for the work you do? Is it hard to identify this? Why or why not?

6. Can you think of situations where God has used your work to refine Christian character?

7. Does your work endure? How does this affect the way you see it?

8. Where do you see the enemy evident in your place of work? Does it help to be aware of this? Why or why not?

9. What spiritual gifts can be exercised in your place of work?

10. In your experience, do you see evidence of a sacred-secular divide? How might we respond to this?

Presence

1. Have you had a sense of God's presence in your place of work? What happened?

2. What for you is the greatest hindrance when it comes to experiencing the presence of God in the workplace?

3. Is God's presence in our places of work ever disruptive? Why or why not?

4. Who in your workplace are you most likely to encounter: Father, Son or Holy Spirit? How might this understanding change when viewed alongside Scripture?

5. Jesus taught his disciples from the boat (their place of work). What do you think Jesus might be teaching you about your work?

6. What spiritual gift is most needed in your workplace at this time?

7. What spiritual fruit (see Galatians 5:22-23) is most needed at this moment?

8. What do you think the Holy Spirit is already doing in your place of work?

9. What practically can you do to recognise the presence of God in your workplace?

Partnership

1. God initiated the partnership with Adam. Why do you think he did this?

2. Is the idea of partnering with God a new or familiar idea to you?

3. What could partnership with God look like for you in your place of work?

4. What issues are important to you in your place of work? How might you partner with God in these areas?

5. Can you give examples where God has provided for you in your place of work?

6. How important to you is a balance of work and rest? How do you maintain this in practice?

7. In your place of work, what examples can you think of where you had to partner with others on their agenda? How did you respond? What did you learn from it?

8. How might we as Christians listen to the Holy Spirit promptings in our places of work?

If you would like to discuss the issues raised in this book, you can email dontstealthestaples@gmail.com

Bibliography

Arnott, John and Carol, *Grace and Forgiveness* (New Wine Press, 2009).

Baer, Michael R., *Breaking Down the Sacred-Secular Divide: A Return to Biblical Thinking in the Church* (CreateSpace Independent Publishing Platform, 2017).

Beckett, John D., *Loving Monday, Succeeding in Business Without Selling Your Soul* (IVP, 2001).

Beckett, John D., *Mastering Monday* (IVP, 2006).

Bell, Dick, *To the Source of the Yangtze* (Hodder & Stoughton Religious, 1991).

Boland, John W., *Workplace Evangelism: Taking Your Faith to Work,* (Tate Publishing, 2012).

Buxton, Graham, *Celebrating Life: Beyond the Sacred-Secular Divide* (Authentic Media, 2007).

Byron, William J., *Answers from Within: Spiritual Guidelines for Managing Setbacks in Work and Life,* (McMillan, 1998).

Campbell, Regi, *About My Father's Business* (Multnomah Publishers, 2005).

Canfield, Jack and Miller, Jacqueline, *Heart at Work* (McGraw-Hill, 1998).

Comer, John Mark, *The Ruthless Elimination of Hurry: How to Stay Spiritually Alive in the Chaos of the Modern World* (Hodder & Stoughton, 2019).

Cooke, Graham, *Crafted Prayer: The Joy of Always Getting Your Prayers Answered* (Brilliant Book House, 2015).

Cosden, Darrell, *The Heavenly Good of Earthly Work* (Paternoster Press, 2006).

Crum, Dr W. Paul, *More Than a Job: Your 24/7 Mission* (Bridge-Logos, 2006).

Curran, Peter, *All the Hours God Sends? Practical and Biblical Help in Meeting the Demands of Work* (IVP, 2000).

Davies, Jon (ed.), *God and the Marketplace: Essays on the Morality of Wealth Creation* (IEA Health and Welfare Unit, 1993).

Dow, Graham, *A Christian Understanding of Daily Work* (Grove Books Ltd, 2000).

Dunn, Ron, *When Heaven is Silent* (CLC, 2008).

Gazelka, Paul, *Marketplace Ministers: Awakening God's People in the Workplace to Their Ultimate Purpose* (Creation House Press, 2003).

Green, Rodney, *90,000 Hours: Managing the World of Work* (Scripture Union, 2002).

Greene, Mark, *Fruitfulness on the Frontline: Making a Difference Where You Are* (IVP, 2014).

Greene, Mark, *Thank God it's Monday* (Scripture Union, 1997).

Greene, Mark, *The One About . . . 8 Stories About God in Our Everyday* (LICC, 2018).

Greene, Mark, *The Great Divide* (LICC, 2013).

Grudem, Wayne, *Systematic Theology* (Zondervan Academic, 1994).

Gentile, Mary C., *Giving Voice to Values: How to Speak Your Mind When You Know What is Right* (Yale University Press, 2010).

Hargreaves, Sam and Sara, *Whole Life Worship* (IVP, 2017).

Hasson, Bob with Silk, Danny *The Business of Honour: Restoring the Heart of Business* (Loving On Purpose, 2017).

Heidebrecht, Paul H., *God's Man in the Marketplace: The Story of Herbert J. Taylor* (IVP, 1990).

Higginson, Richard, *Questions of Business Life: Exploring Workplace Issues from a Christian Perspective* (Spring Harvest Publishing Division and Authentic Media, 2002).

Hillman, Os, *Faith and Work: Do They Mix? Discovering God's Purpose for Your Work* (Aslan Group Publishing, 2000).

Humphreys, Tony, *Work and Worth: Take Back Your Life* (Newleaf, 2002).

Hybels, Bill, *Christians in the Marketplace: Making Your Faith Work in the Secular World* (Hodder & Stoughton, 1993).

Johnson, Bill, *Dreaming with God: Secrets to Redesigning Your World Through God's Creative Flow* (Destiny Image Publishers Inc., 2006).

Johnson, Bill, *The Resting Place* (Destiny Image Publishers Inc., 2019).

Jones, Timothy, *Workday Prayers: On the Job Meditations for Tending Your Soul* (Loyala Press, 2000).

Keller, Timothy, *Every Good Endeavour: Connecting Your Work to God's Work* (Penguin, 2012).

Kellet, David, *Champions for God at Work* (TerraNova Publications, 2001).

Kendal, R.T., *Jealousy: The Sin No-one Talks About* (Hodder & Stoughton, 2011).

Kendal, R.T., *Total Forgiveness* (Hodder & Stoughton, 2003).

Latham, Don, *A Faith That Works* (Terra Nova Publications Ltd, 1997).

Lawrence, Brother, *The Practice of the Presence of God* (Leyland Edwards, 2018).

Lencioni, Patrick, *The Five Dis-functions of a Team* (John Wiley & Sons, 2002).

Lencioni, Patrick, *Silos, Politics and Turf Wars* (Jossey-Bass, 2006).

Livingstone Smith, David, *Less than Human: Why We Demean, Enslave and Exterminate Others* (St Martin's Press, 2011).

Lowry, Kevin, *Faith at Work: Finding Purpose Beyond the Paycheck* (Kevin Lowry, 2012).

Marshall, Rich, *God @ Work: Discovering the Anointing for Business* (Destiny Image, 2000).

Miller, David W., *God at Work: The History and Promise of the Faith at Work Movement* (Oxford University Press, 2007).

Muir, John G., *More Than My Job's Worth: Meeting Challenges to Faith* (Christian Focus Publications Ltd, 1993).

Nash, Laura and McLennan, Scotty, *Church on Sunday, Work on Monday: The Challenge of Fusing Christian Values with Business Life* (Jossey-Bass, 2001).

Noble, Alan, *Disruptive Witness: Speaking Truth in a Distracted Age* (IVP Books, 2018).

Oliver, David and Thwaites, James, *Church That Works* (Word Publishing, 2001).

Oliver, David, *Work, Prison or Place of Destiny?* (Word Publishing, 2000).

Peabody, Larry, *Secular Work is Full-time Service* (Christian Literature Crusade, 1974).

Peel, Bill and Larimore, Walt, *Workplace Grace* (LeTourneau Press, 2014).

Purbrick, Lorraine, *Shift Direction: Find Your Way to the Job You Love* (Verité CM Ltd, 2016).

Reed, Esther D., *Good Work: Christian Ethics in the Workplace* (Baylor University Press, 2010).

Richardson, Alan, *The Biblical Doctrine of Work* (SCM Press Ltd, 1954).

Ruberi, Jani, *More Than a Job: Creating a Portfolio Lifestyle* (Spring Harvest Publication Division and Paternoster Lifestyle, 2001).

Schumacher, Christian, *God in Work* (Lion Publishing, 1998).

Seamands, David, *Healing for Damaged Emotions* (David C. Cook Publishing Company, 2019).

Shattock, Geoff, *Wake Up to Work: Friendship and Faith in the Workplace* (Scripture Union, 1999).

Sheppard, David, Allcock, James and Innes, Robert, *God at Work (Part II)* (Grove Books Ltd, 1995).

Shearer, Darren, *The Marketplace Christian: A Practical Guide to Using Your Spiritual Gifts in Business*, Kindle Edition (High Bridge Books, 2015).

Sherman, Doug and Hendricks, William, *Your Work Matters to God* (NavPress, 1987).

Silvoso, Ed, *Anointed for Business: How Christians Can Use Their Influence in the Marketplace to Change the World* (Regal Books, 2002).

Silvoso, Ed, *Transformation: Change the Marketplace and You Change the World* (Chosen Books, 2007).

Stevens, R. Paul, *Doing God's Business* (Wm. B. Eerdmans Publishing Co., 2006).

Stevens, R. Paul and Ung, Alvin, *Taking Your Soul to Work: Overcoming the Nine Deadly Sins of the Workplace* (Wm. B. Eerdmans Publishing Co., 2010).

Stevens, R. Paul, *Work Matters: Lessons from Scripture* (Wm. B. Eerdmans Publishing Co., 2012).

Turley, Joan L., *Sacred Work in Secular Places* (Author Academy Elite, 2017).

Veith, Gene Edward, Jr, *God at Work, Your Christian Vocation in All of Life* (Crossway Books, 2021).

Westacott, David, *Work Well, Live Well: Rediscovering a Biblical View of Work* (Marshall Pickering, 1996).

Williamson, Roy, *Wholly Alive: Integrating Faith and Everyday life* (SPCK, 2003).

Wynne, Jago, *Working Without Wilting: Starting Well to Finish Strong* (IVP, 2009).

Zigarelli, Michael A., *Faith at Work* (Moody Press, 2000).

Acknowledgements

I am grateful to God's continued presence throughout my working life. He has given me purpose in the various roles I have undertaken. Through my work he has provided for both the needs of others and the financial needs of my family. He has always been faithful to his promises.

I wish also to thank and acknowledge those who kindly reviewed the book and gave feedback: David Butler, Josh Coleman, Stephen Coleman, Josh Cutting, Philip Dolby, David Eastwood, Sam Evans, John Lovell, Tim Maiden, Andy Marshall, Lydia Rolley, Mick Rolley, Mike Rutter, John White, Lisa Wilson and Pete Wynter.

I wish also to acknowledge the artist for all illustrations, appearing under the handle 'charcoal_x' from www.Fiverr.com.

Finally, my thanks go to Margaret, my wife, who proof-read the various manuscripts as well as providing invaluable feedback and encouragement.